To Mike —

Thank you for
all that you do!

Here's
all my best

PINOT ROCKS

PINOT ROCKS

A WINDING JOURNEY THROUGH *INTENSE* ELEGANCE

MICHAEL BROWNE

LIONCREST

PUBLISHING

PINOT ROCKS

A Winding Journey through Intense Elegance

ISBN   978-1-5445-1501-4   *Hardcover*

978-1-5445-1499-4   *Paperback*

978-1-5445-1500-7   *Ebook*

978-1-5445-1502-1   *Audiobook*

To my wife, Sarah

Logan, Lauren, Lyvia

S.

L.L.L.

CONTENTS

CHAPTER 1

CHILDHOOD

MY DAD WAS ORIGINALLY FROM BOSTON, MY MOM from Utah, but they both wound up in the Bay Area, which is where they met. My dad went to San Jose State for undergrad and then got his master's in entomology at Berkeley. My father enjoyed his time in San Francisco, but grew tired of city life; he spent his summers as a child with his brother George in Humboldt County and really enjoyed that. So when I was four, we moved to the small town of Wenatchee in Washington State, where my dad got a job as a research scientist at Washington State University's Tree Fruit Research Center. That's where I grew up.

I had a tough upbringing in some respects. My mom was brilliant, but she was also troubled in some areas of her life. This was before there was much understanding of what her condition was or how to treat or help her. It was difficult to live with her. Although she was very loving, she had her own battles to deal with.

When I was a little kid, she would always ask me if someone had been in our house. She thought someone was making a mess in my room, and she acted very paranoid. One time I couldn't tell her who had been in our house—because to my knowledge, no one had been in it—and she poured a bowl of milk on my head because she thought I was lying to her. I was confused and afraid a lot. I had no idea what my mom was talking about, or what I could do to make things better.

My parents had an interesting, tumultuous relationship. They fought frequently. It seemed they were always yelling. I remember one time, lying in bed listening to an intense fight, and I felt like I couldn't take it anymore. I went upstairs and told the two of them to shut up. I did not know what else to do. I was eight years old.

I didn't know how to deal with that. I just wanted a peaceful home, and I didn't understand what was going on. It was stressful, it was tough, and I didn't have anyone to go to who could help me understand and deal with this.

I would isolate myself, unknowingly, and look at other families that seemed normal, not understanding why we were different. It was a tough time. I had a hard time navigating friendships and other relationships. I think that was based on my fear; I didn't want people to see my mom as she was because I had no idea how to explain it, or her, or what my house was like.

I can see now as an adult how alone I was, especially with school. They were not involved in my school activities too much, whether it was "show your art" day or anything like that. It was not that they were not involved, they just had their own things going on and they were doing the best they could.

I look back on this now and it seems almost unreal. I had no idea how crazy things were at the time. You don't really know any different when you're a kid.

Even though the fighting was awful between my parents, they never fought with me or my sister. My dad was very active in our lives, outside of school. He took us hunting, fishing, and to gun clubs. He was an active participant in that part of our lives. My mom was more of an observer.

I think because she was having such a hard time navigating her world, my mom began spinning out of control. She left us when I was in fifth grade (ten years old), and moved back to San Mateo, California, with her mother. From that point forward, I didn't really have an active mother in my life until my father got remarried when I was fourteen.

That was so hard. My friends would say, "Ask your mom if

you can come over to play." I would say, "I have to ask my dad, and he's not home yet." They didn't get it. "Why can't you just ask your mom and play now?" They didn't get it, and I had a hard time saying that my mom wasn't around.

With that said, it was a relief that she was in a different state. It relaxed our household, and I didn't have to deal with the fighting and unpredictability of her being around.

A friend came over one day; he was walking down my street, crying, just after my parents got divorced. I asked him what was wrong. He was devastated that his parents got divorced. And I told him I was so relieved that my parents got divorced, and I was excited about it. I didn't know any different; I was excited about this reprieve from those stressful times. And I realized further that my situation was just not normal, which only added to my lack of confidence and my confusion.

My dad was an introvert, and he didn't know how to handle the heartbreak. He shut down. I invited him to go out with me on many occasions, but he frequently declined. He was still there for me, and he was still a good dad, but looking back, he was obviously depressed. I can't blame him. It must have been very hard to deal with.

For a while, he became more lax in his parenting and wasn't motivated to do much. Looking back now, he was under a lot of pressure to raise two kids as a single father. I can remember more than a few times, I asked him to throw the ball around. He would decline, and I would throw the ball against the house by myself. That happened a lot after Mom left. I felt very alone and didn't have a lot of direction in life at that point. I was left to my own devices to navigate a lot of my world as a kid. Since my dad did the same when he was a kid, and grew up in a time when you could wander the streets of San Francisco, I guess he thought that was the way kids operated. He wasn't necessarily inattentive; he was responsible, but he was just not that active in some parts of our lives. I did enjoy the freedom, though.

I was sad for him because I saw the sadness within him. He was a loving dad and did the best he could, but those times were very hard on him, and he was just trying to do what he had to do in order to provide a stable home for the two of us, which he did.

My dad came around after a while, and it was a relief when we started to do some of the fun things we used to do. He was a stable presence in my life.

For activities, we gravitated toward what he was interested in, which was mainly outdoor activities like hunting, fishing, and camping, which I also liked. Those times were enjoyable. I still enjoy those activities and feel grateful that we had those times together and that I learned so much from him.

However, his guidance didn't stop me from making a lot of foolish decisions in my adolescence.

PLAYING WITH FIRE

My dad and I were into muzzleloader rifles and guns. We attended primitive rendezvous, where people wore buckskins, hung out in teepees, and rode horses. Very cool for a kid.

There were shooting competitions at these rendezvous. My dad had cut down a 50-caliber rifle for me, and I used it in children's competitions. He always instructed me to use no more than fifty grains of gunpowder (fifty grains is about a medium measurement of powder, and I could get a good thirty-five-yard shot with it).

The memory of this one shooting competition is still vivid in my mind. I had a special powder horn that my dad had made for me, which I still have to this day. It was a cow horn with an intricate scrimshaw of an eagle on it. It had a tiny point on it that would open the powder-measuring device and measure the quantity. I measured out fifty grains. Then my young mind thought, if fifty grains is good, wouldn't 150 be better? I had experimented with about seventy-five to a hundred grains before, so why not increase that amount?

My dad had warned me that too much powder could blow up the gun, but I wanted to see what would happen with 150.

In the third round of the competition, I loaded 150 grains into my rifle. Boom! The sound was deafening. Everyone was looking around, trying to find the source of the explosion. All they saw was a cloud of smoke and no one there, because it blew me back a few feet.

My dad came over, looked at me, and said, "I told you, only fifty grains. Don't ever do that again. Now you see what can happen—you got lucky."

Not sure what I learned from that, because I made some more dumb mistakes with things that explode.

In another shooting competition, I won a spool of cannon fuse.

My dad was cool with it, but he told me, "Just make sure you don't break it, because if you break it, then you light it, it will probably go out in the middle, and then you have to be really careful because you have to track it for a relight."

I decided I wanted to test this theory one afternoon when I was home alone to see if it stopped. I decided I would crack it after a foot, and if it didn't stop, I'd just put it out with water. What could go wrong?

I cracked the coil, and the fuse grew just like the one in the intro to *Mission Impossible*. The flame didn't stop after the break.

I panicked.

Now I had an actual *Mission Impossible* situation to deal with.

Now it was time for plan B. I put the coil underneath the faucet and turned the water on. To my horror, the water spread the flame instead of extinguishing and ignited the entire coil in one big flash.

Mind you, cannon fuse is loaded with gunpowder, so it is highly volatile. It quickly started burning my hand, so I freaked out and reacted by throwing the coil onto the carpet.

The fuse broke apart as I threw it and landed on the carpet in a dozen or more semicircles. The flames kept going and burned our 1970s polyester carpet. My hand was scorched and covered in huge blisters. It was a total disaster. I couldn't hide this one.

I didn't know what else to do at that point, so I called my dad. I told him I had the coil in my hand while something was cooking on the stove. Somehow, the red-hot burner ignited the coil.

He believed me, and I didn't get in trouble. But I still hadn't learned my lesson.

I grew up in what I thought was a very good neighborhood.

I had a lot of friends in the houses surrounding me, and five of us were named Mike. Our parents numbered us to keep track. I was Mike Number Three. I can still hear my dad calling out, "Mike Three, time for dinner!"

Three out of the Five Mikes were good friends, and I was one of them. We ran around apple orchards, climbed cherry trees, walked around our town and neighborhood, and spent a lot of time outdoors. One day, Mike One and I were messing around and bored, and I asked him if he wanted to light some black powder. He had no idea what that was. In the garage, we had this cabinet full of black powder (for our muzzleloader rifles), so I found a small plastic cocktail cup and filled it up.

There was a lot of powder in there, but as far as I knew, black powder was just for show and flash. I didn't think we could do much damage. I put a bunch of buckshot in the cup for extra effect.

Another Mike, Mike Four, who we didn't really hang out with, lived next door to me. We didn't like him much at that time because he was a bit older, big, and used his size to beat us at basketball and other neighborhood games. I remember his parents were anal about cleanliness. They never let any of us in their house, and we didn't see them very often.

So there we were, in the middle of our street in our subdivision at three thirty in the afternoon, trying to ignite black powder in a cup. We didn't have a fuse, since I burned it up on a previous occasion, so we were just flicking matches at it. Just then, Mike Four got off the school bus. He asked us what we were doing. We told him we were trying to light black powder. He offered to light it. I said "Sure, go ahead. It's easy."

We gave him the matches and stood back. He hovered over the cup and dropped a lit match right into the middle of the cup.

WHOOSH!

His head was engulfed in smoke, and we saw a rush of flames. His hair and eyebrows were singed, burning and smoking. He ran into his house—which we'd never been in before— and we ran in after him.

Mike Four ran down the hallway to his bathroom, leaving a trail of smoke behind him. His hair was still smoldering with that distinctive smell of singed hair.

I was sure Mike One and I were dead—Mike Four's parents were going to kill us. Mike One and I tried not to freak out. Mike Four was looking at himself in the mirror when his mom came home.

We panicked and made up a story: we told her a car drove

by, threw something out the window, and it blew up in Mike Four's face. She called the police, and then rushed out of the house with Mike Four in tow. She yelled out that they were going to the hair salon to cut out the singed hair.

I wondered why the emergency room was not a better option, but I guess because he had no burns or injuries other than an impromptu redo of the hairdo.

We stood in Mike Four's hallway with our mouths wide open as she drove off. We tried to figure out what to tell the police when they arrived.

Two patrol cars showed up a few minutes later. I thought I was going to crap my pants. Mike One and I stuck to the original story about the drive-by minibomb. Somehow, I was the lead communicator in this deal, so I had to make up details. I told the police there were five people in the car. I said it was very similar to a station wagon that was parked down the street. They asked the color, and I pointed to another car. After all of their questions, I ended up describing a pea-green station wagon with several people in it. I told them I wasn't able to identify anyone from the car because they were driving too fast.

The police asked for the device, and I reluctantly brought out the evidence I had since hidden in my garage. The police could tell there was melted buckshot in the gnarly-looking leftovers.

Police: "It looks like a crude device."

Well no kidding, dude, it was made by a ten-year-old!

I didn't say that; I just stuck to the story. I kept wondering what consequences awaited me if and when Mike Four (or Two) spilled the beans on us. Would my dad hang me from a tree, or would he be more creative than that? Boiled by oil? Drawn and quartered? I had no idea.

My dad came home and nothing happened that night. The next day, he pulled out the newspaper and told me to look at the front page: "Boy's Hair Singed by Flying Bomb." He read the story out loud, and it was almost verbatim what I'd told the police. He told me to take it to class to read (which was the daily practice at my school).

The police bought it! And a reporter bought it!

Most importantly, my dad bought it. And neither Mike One nor Mike Four ever spilled the beans, because they didn't want to die by torture either. We were in the clear.

You would think I would have learned my lesson right then and there: no more explosives. But I was a kid, and I was still curious. I continued my experiments with black powder.

In junior high, I started hanging out with a different group of friends. This group had similar experiences as me, and we kinda ran around and did what we wanted to do. I was in eighth grade in middle school. We weren't the best students and kinda stayed on the outside of the rest of the social groups.

We hung out at Ed's house a lot because his mom worked a lot and we could do whatever we wanted. One night, while bored at his house, I thought it would be a good idea to light some black powder, and maybe this time have it make a sound instead of just a flash.

We went to my house and retrieved some black powder and returned to Ed's house. We didn't have a container, so we snooped around his sister's room and found a small glass bottle of clear nail polish. We dumped the contents of the bottle and started planning our experiment. We packed the bottle with black powder and stepped outside. Ed's house was right at the corner of the apple orchard, so we had plenty of room. We didn't have any firecrackers to use as a fuse, so I decided to light the bottom of the bottle. Man, would that spool of canon fuse come in handy right then. Since nail polish remover was flammable, and I figured it would be slow-burning, that could double as a fuse.

I lit the bottle at the bottom where some of the polish had spilled out. Perfect plan. The issue was that a few grains of the black powder had stuck to the polish. That turned out to be a very fast and aggressive fuse. It exploded immediately. Glass shrapnel went flying, severing a vein in my hand and shredding my fingers up. Blood spurted everywhere.

It was wintertime—there was snow on the ground, so as my hand was spraying blood, it was getting all over the snow. It looked like a hawk had eaten a really big chicken.

Ed's mom freaked out and started screaming; blood was all over the kitchen, and my finger was still squirting blood everywhere. She called my dad, but that was not enough for me. I demanded that we go to the emergency room. On the way, I tried to devise a story to get away with this so I wouldn't get in trouble. I had visions of prison camps and forced marches in my head.

Later, I told my dad we used a bottle as a stand for an old firework, and the fuse went off too quickly. His response: "You gotta watch those old fireworks."

I have since told him the true story of each of these, but I did it over time, to make sure I didn't have to go to any prison camps or endure any torture.

SCHOOL DAZE

As a kid, I didn't just blow things up. I had to cope with my mom's leaving and navigate the academic and social aspects of school.

In elementary school, I shied away from most social contact, even though I wasn't exactly a loner. I had friends but didn't run with the "in crowd." I was always on the fringe.

For example, in my community, everyone was expected to play football (or other sports). I played for a little while but didn't like it. It's not that I didn't like being part of a team. I did. I just didn't like football, or the coaches, or the whole structure, and honestly, I didn't make a contribution to the team. I wasn't a good athlete, and everything I did was minimal. So I quit whatever sport I started.

In retrospect, I quit because I was self-conscious, and I quit because I didn't learn the value of hard work, self-sacrifice, and dedication. Looking back, I wish I had stuck with it. But at the time I felt like too much of an outsider, and I didn't understand why I would keep doing this thing I didn't like. Also, I didn't want to expose my weaknesses.

I also didn't want to be like everyone else. That was also a part of me. I didn't want to be with the crowd; I wanted to forge my own path. A lot of kids wanted to follow the in-crowd and do what the popular kids did. I could feel the tension and struggle as everyone tried so hard to fit in. Fitting in just wasn't for me. I liked the road less traveled.

I was more comfortable with that, and it made more sense to me. I didn't care what other people did; I was cool doing my own thing. But at the same time, I did care what people thought. It was a conflict.

The pressure to fit in became even greater once I started high school. School became a big cliché. There were different cliques and groups of people, with the athletes and jocks as the stars of the show. I didn't want any part of that. In eighth grade I became withdrawn and did my own thing, and that continued in high school. "My own thing" was hanging out with my friends on the fringe, running around town, and dabbling in a bit of weed and alcohol, which wasn't my thing but that's what they did so I did it as well. Another conflict, but those were my friends and I enjoyed their friendship.

My dad was not just an entomologist. He was also a skilled craftsman. He would fashion breathtaking pieces of Native American artwork, as well as gun work and woodwork, and could also work with metal. His work always involved the highest level of detail, which was something that intrigued me and that I had so much respect for. His shop was messy, yet organized at the same time. Not one screwdriver was out of place, and all flatheads faced the same direction. I think part of the mess was having two kids, because now his shop is immaculate.

Seeing my dad making these beautiful pieces made me want

to become a craftsman. I discovered the satisfaction of turning raw material into a finished product. My creativity kicked in. I wanted to make things.

My newfound interest became a big part of my life in high school. When we went hunting, I'd gather feathers so I could use them when I tied flies for fly-fishing. I had learned how to do this in one of my PE classes. I would go to antique shops with my dad and buy old pieces of furniture so I could refinish them. One of my favorite pastimes was me in my basement, refinishing anything I could get my hands on. I blasted Def Leppard and Nazareth on my tape deck as I stripped, sanded, and stained. I analyzed the grain of wood and tested different stains on each piece until I was happy with it.

I never sold any of the furniture I refinished. I gave it away to friends or used it. We had craft fairs, so I was able to sell other items I had made. Pieces of leather with pheasant feathers and beads on it, which I called "hat clips," were bestsellers. They were actually roach clips for blunts, although I didn't really know that at the time. Sometimes stoner girls called and asked to buy hat clips. I found it very amusing. One of them told me, "That's not a hat clip; that's a roach clip." And she explained to me, and I got it. They would spend five dollars to buy something that cost me about a dollar to make. I liked that.

High school was boring for me. I wasn't a good student, and I didn't like the teaching style of that day. The teachers seemed like robots in front of the class. I didn't care for many subjects, either, except for Shakespeare. Shakespeare was interesting, mainly because the teacher kept us engaged. We arranged our chairs in a circle and we were all involved in the learning process. Every student participated and had something meaningful to say. I remember absorbing each student's interpretation of Macbeth. Shakespeare was a bright spot for me in school because of the teaching style and the engagement of the group.

I also liked business classes and especially enjoyed a group called DECA. DECA was a marketing and entrepreneurship association for students. The teacher was creative, dynamic, goofy, and engaging. He wasn't like the typical boring teacher, like my typing teacher. I skipped typing class for four months because I could just not take the teacher's style. He was kind of a jerk as well.

My typing teacher had a conversation with the DECA teacher about my chronic absence. My typing teacher thought I had moved out of the area or changed schools. We ended up making a pretty sweet deal. I would help out in the school store, and in exchange they wouldn't tell my dad I had been skipping class.

I learned a lot about business in general. I liked that being creative was essential. Through my experience in DECA, I started to realize that I didn't want to go and work for a business. I wanted to build one. The curriculum focused on writing business plans, and research and development. We also learned about business management. To me, building a business was a natural evolutionary process, and I could wrap my head around it. It all made sense.

My passion for the organization led me to run for regional president. I had no idea how to be a leader, but I thought jumping into it, trial by fire, would be the best way to learn. I had no idea what to do; I was in a rush and a hurry, so I did the best I could. I made a big poster for my election for the cafeteria, and I'm a bad speller anyway.

After two days, this one kid asked me:

"Michael, what's wrong with your sign?"

I said, "What do you mean, man? Nothing is wrong with it."

"You misspelled 'president.'"

"No I didn't."

"Where's the I?"

And then I saw it. It said: "Michael Browne for Presdent."

I'm pretty sure everyone noticed, but nobody said anything about it until after the sign had been up for two days.

Despite the spelling error, I thought I had a good chance of winning the election. That is, until my campaign manager, always the comedian, messed things up big time.

I was boarding a bus that was taking us to another school for a DECA election debate. I was mortified when I saw flyers everywhere that blatantly insulted my opponent. They said things like, "Amanda is an idiot, vote for Michael Browne."

Oh no, dude, that is a misfire!

My campaign manager had created these flyers and placed them all over the bus. I told him to take the flyers down, and to pick up the loose ones that were strewn all over the floor. He said everything would be fine, but I argued with him and demanded he get rid of them.

By that time, it was too late. Too many people had seen the flyers. I lost the election. I lost not due to the flyers, but due to my lack of preparation.

I was pretty devastated, especially because I thought I could have won. I put a lot of work into the election, and it stung to know I lost because I wasn't prepared. I didn't prepare for the debate, I rushed the sign, and I didn't have a clear vision for my campaign manager to make good signs. Of course I lost. That was a hard loss because I looked like a fool doing it.

The disappointment was heavy, but it didn't last long. I realized I had done something I had never done before. I gave my all to something. I did my best. Yes, losing the election hurt. But I learned that if I was going to conquer a big task, I needed to be prepared, take ownership, and bust my ass.

I got through the rest of high school by the skin of my teeth. When I was a junior, my friends were seniors, so they had three periods instead of seven. I skipped my remaining four periods to hang out with my fringe buddies. Due to my junior year truancy, I had to kick it into high gear as a senior to graduate. I wanted to be done with school, so I did it.

I graduated high school on time, but just barely. I almost didn't believe I made it.

CHAPTER 2

KID WORK

I KNEW I WANTED TO MAKE MONEY AT AN EARLY AGE. When I was thirteen, a friend told me he worked at a Chinese restaurant. He was sure they would hire me, so I put in an application. The owner was adamant that I have a Social Security card before I started working there. I told him I would apply for a card, and that sealed the deal. I earned $3.35 per hour as a dishwasher and moved up to cutting vegetables in no time. This was better than my five dollars a week allowance at home.

About three weeks into the job, the owner asked to see my Social Security card. I told him I hadn't received it yet. Since I didn't have it on me, he had to let me go. We came to an agreement that I would quit for a while, and then return when I could show him the card.

I got a phone call from him a few days later. It was high school graduation night. All of his busboys were seniors, so none of them could work. He asked me if I could bus tables. I jumped at the opportunity. I bused tables and watched customers like a hawk, making sure I kept their water glasses full. I earned $14.35 in cash for three hours of work. That was exciting.

I worked as a busboy for a little while longer and then got a job at the nursing home where my stepmother worked. I earned $7.50 per hour. I helped out in the dining room, along with a couple of other people. Sometimes, we would help the chef. It was easy work in a laid-back environment. I enjoyed it. I worked there three nights per week for about a year.

Once I started getting a steady paycheck in my hand, I became obsessed with working and making money.

CONTROLLING MY DESTINY

I didn't like school, but I liked learning, and I started reading everything I could about the American Dream. I read books, articles, anything that caught my eye. I gravitated toward stories that embodied the American Dream—building something from nothing.

I enjoyed reading entrepreneur biographies and how-to

books. I wanted to learn all I could about successful people. Where did their ideas come from? What inspired them? How did they pitch their ideas to potential investors? How did they deal with adversity? What was their background? How did they do it? I wanted to develop their mindset.

The funny thing was, at that point I wasn't quite sure what my goal was. I just knew it involved making money and building a business. I didn't read entrepreneurial magazines because they were heavily focused on franchising. I didn't read finance books or magazines either. I wanted to learn the process of starting a business. I moved on to reading about creating business plans (which is a big part of why I loved DECA so much in high school). It was really important to me to start something from nothing and build it myself.

I don't know why I had such a strong interest in entrepreneurship and the American Dream. I was only thirteen. Most thirteen-year olds were reading comic books, but I was learning how to become an entrepreneur. Why did I have the desire to achieve financial security and success?

I've thought about this a lot since then. I think it was because I wanted to provide for my family in the future. I didn't want them to worry about money. I wanted them to have more than I had.

I wanted to do something creative in my life. I wanted to

build something, to create something, something no one else had ever done. That's what all these entrepreneurs did; they risked and failed and eventually succeeded, and that was very exciting to me.

Growing up, my dad provided very well, but things could have been better. For example, I had only one pair of jeans in seventh grade. If I wanted something, we didn't have money lying around. I had to work and save.

I remember saving for a pair of white Nike shoes with a red stripe on them. They were just like the ones that John Ritter wore on *Three's Company*. I thought they were the coolest shoes and I had to have them. I worked hard, saved my money, and made the purchase.

I was so proud when I wore them to school the next day. There was a problem, though. A bunch of guys asked me why I was wearing cheerleader shoes.

I had no idea what they were talking about. Apparently a rival school's cheerleading team wore the exact same shoes, same color, everything.

I never wore them again.

It was frustrating to have saved up all that money, only to throw the shoes in the back of my closet. It hurt. It wasn't even being made fun of—what hurt was that I had worked so hard to get cool new shoes, and now I had to go back to my ratty old sneakers.

If my kids wanted shoes, I wanted to be able to buy them as many shoes as they wanted.

I often saw my dad with bills spread out on our table, budgeting for various things and working hard to make sure it all worked. It seemed so sad to me. I overheard conversations between my dad and his friends. Some of them would talk about work like it was a prison sentence. They would say things like: "Well, I have fifteen more years on the job," or, "Only six more years until retirement."

I wondered why they continued with a job they didn't like. I don't think any of them hated it, but they didn't seem to enjoy it either. I didn't want to deal with those frustrations. I didn't see a life like that as very appealing to me. Nothing at all wrong with it, just not my cup of tea.

And they talked about retirement in terms of Social Security, and how that wasn't enough to live off of. I remember wondering why they hadn't saved more. I wrote off Social Security as a kid and remember thinking to myself that I'd never want to live like that.

My dad's friends looked forward to their hobbies, such as

hunting and golfing. It seemed like they were working for the weekend. That was fine for them, but I was striving for more. I didn't want only two out of seven days of the week to bring me fulfillment. I didn't want my job to feel like work; I wanted to enjoy it—and I wanted to make plenty of money doing it.

I told my dad one day that I wanted to someday build a business and become financially secure. He said he could be a millionaire if he wanted to, but it wasn't his game. He knew what becoming a millionaire entailed, and he preferred not to do it. That's cool, I had respect for him for that. There is no doubt that he could have done it if he wanted since he is brilliant. But that lifestyle was not for him, and he knew it.

I told him it was my game, and I was going for it. I didn't want to settle for a third of my income at retirement. I wanted financial security.

Not every example that spurred me on to success was negative. My dad's friend, Don, owned an apple packing business. He had a nice home. His kitchen always smelled of good food. His family seemed almost perfect. His kids were very polite. They never acted like they were better than anyone else because they had money. They had a well-balanced life, with lots of spare time to do the things they enjoyed.

I looked up to Don and his family. What were they doing differently than other people?

The answer was clear: they had their own business.

They had a secure, steady income, and they weren't chained to a job they disliked. They didn't have to rely on anyone else.

I wanted to become more like that. I wanted to control my destiny.

FLAMBÉS AT THE THUNDERBIRD

My friend, Glenn, worked at the Thunderbird, the only high-end restaurant in town at the time. I saw him doing well, and I decided I wanted to work there. It would be an opportunity for me to meet and observe wealthy, successful people. My dad was fine with me working there, as long as I kept my grades up.

I got a job there as a busboy. I made $25 to $30 each night, which was good money back then. I had to wear a puffy, brown, polyester shirt as part of the uniform, but it was worth it.

I excelled in my busboy duties, and the manager noticed. He told me he wanted to make me a captain, which meant I would actually be doing the flambés and making way more money. There was a problem: I was too young. Captains had to be eighteen years old. I was only sixteen at the time.

The manager came up with a plan. He told me to quit and reapply in two months. He instructed me to put a new, false birth date on the next application. He would rehire me as an eighteen-year-old.

So I got a job as a cashier at Payless (which was like a Rite Aid or Walgreens). I cut down boxes and did other mundane tasks. It was awful. I kept reminding myself it was only temporary. I quit exactly two months later and reapplied at the Thunderbird. I wrote down a random birthdate, and the manager handed my uniform back to me.

Since the manager had faith in my abilities, he treated me like every other captain. As a captain, I made flambés. I wondered what the customers would think if they knew a sixteen-year-old was pouring brandy and lighting fires to cook their food.

My time as captain was really impactful to me. It was the first time I really saw how wealthy people lived, talked, and acted. I watched how customers carried themselves. I listened to their conversations. I observed how they interacted with each other. I learned proper etiquette and the ins and outs of high-end dining. I learned how to correctly pronounce the names of fine wines. Well, only a few of them.

The job also reinforced the importance of having a strong work ethic. I was committed to my job. I did it well, and I was earning a good paycheck. I even had a girlfriend. Life was good.

Then, the Thunderbird hired a new general manager. A few weeks later when I arrived at work, the gal at the front desk asked me to fill out a personal information form. She said the new manager was cleaning house and they couldn't seem to find my application. They needed to update employee records for accuracy. She was strictly business and a bit gruff, kind of like the character in the *Monster's, Inc.* movie that kept the records of all the employees. Great character!

I forgot the random birthdate I had put down on my second application, so I made up another one. The new manager noticed the discrepancy and fired me.

That was the one and only time I was ever fired from a job.

Before I got fired, I dropped by my friend's house where they were having a get together with a bunch of other friends. I said I would see them later and headed off to work. I quickly returned since I was no longer employed and had some free time. When I walked in, I saw my girlfriend on the couch, making out with a good friend of mine.

Without missing a step, I turned on my heel and walked out.

I had lost both my job and my girlfriend within a couple of hours. Not my best day, although I was not too disappointed in either situation, to be honest.

~

CHAPTER 3

~

LIFE IS A CIRCUS

BETWEEN THE AGES OF TWELVE AND EIGHTEEN, I WAS
in the Wenatchee Youth Circus. This wasn't a small-time
circus. They had many of the acts you would expect to see in
a larger circus, including trapeze, high-wire, and fire-breath-
ing. The only thing it didn't really have was the big animals.

One day when I was twelve, my friend, a trapeze artist,
asked me if I wanted to join the circus.

I was intrigued. I always had an admiration for circus per-
formers when I was younger, since we went to the show
many times. The coordination, skill, and practice it took to
do what they did was amazing. I was in awe of people who
were dedicated to their craft.

But clearly, if you wanted to be in this circus, you had to

know how to do things like eat fire, or balance on a high-wire, or ride a unicycle. I told him I had no acrobatic skills and I certainly couldn't breathe fire. The only thing I was good at was refinishing furniture. I didn't see a lot of polished, mahogany chifforobes in their act, you know?

He said it didn't matter. I could start by helping out and see where it led. I wasn't into sports, I liked the circus, and I was bored, so I agreed to try it.

Next thing I knew, I was wearing blue overalls, moving mats, and changing out sets between acts. It was hard, grueling work, but to be honest, I loved it.

I can remember the very first night—I was watching an act finish, getting ready to move something, when I caught myself thinking, "Wow, I'm actually out here. I'm not sitting in the stands." It was a new feeling for me, something I really liked.

It felt good to be included in the group, and I got to see the acts up close. The people were amazing. Parents were involved, and the kids had fun sleepovers at night. The girls slept in a large tent, and the guys slept on the circus lot. We'd take turns sleeping on the trampoline, on mats, or in the nets. We worked hard together, we hung out together, we were like a family.

My circus life and school life were very different. They were two separate worlds, and I liked to keep them that way. In school, we were divided into categories and cliques. In the circus, there was a sense of togetherness. The athletes and the band geeks were united as one. We had the common goal of perfecting our craft and entertaining the masses. We were like a giant baseball team. The circus was one big family. I met a lot of dear friends there, from all walks of life. The circus captured my heart quickly (it still has it today).

I loved the circus, but being a stagehand was not enough for me. I wanted to be on stage performing. At the time, I really liked the unicycle act. Men and women rode in pyramid-style formations, and they did other stunts. After watching the act numerous times, I decided I wanted to do it.

Small problem: I did not know how to ride a unicycle.

Solution: The only way to learn how to ride a unicycle is to practice. I told my parents what I wanted to do, and they bought me a unicycle for Christmas.

I rode it up and down my street for a while, but that got old. Then I started riding it around town. I needed to practice on hills and curbs, and get a feel for maneuvering the unicycle on different terrains. I went downtown often. I even rode the unicycle to my job at the Chinese restaurant. Sometimes my coworkers would tease me. Around town, I became known as the "guy on the unicycle." The people in my town were not so inventive with nicknames.

I mastered riding the unicycle, and I became a member of the act. After participating for about a year, I thought it was time to learn more skills. Next, I wanted to learn how to eat and breathe fire. That always got my attention during the shows, and I thought it was amazing (yes, I wanted to do this despite my previous mishaps with explosives).

The costumes for the fire act were really cool. My step-mother, Sharon, made my costume for me. She put so much work into that. I wish I still had it. The costumes were a sleek black, and had flames on them. This made the act even more appealing. I was a driven young teen, so I accomplished my goal in no time. I was in the fire act not long after I started my training.

The second year I was in the act, we found out the television show, *That's Incredible!*, was doing a feature on our youth circus. We were giddy with anticipation. No one from our little town that we knew of had ever been on television before. This was a big deal. The team was pumped up for *That's Incredible!*, and we put in extra practice to make sure our act would be on point. At that time, the biggest act I was in was the fire act.

Filming day arrived, and the whole high school baseball stadium was packed. They had scaffolding up with these big cameras and all the trucks and everything. One problem: the wind was seriously gusting. Unforgiving.

We were kind of leery of performing the fire act that day. I mean, when you are blowing fire around, wind is not your friend. However, we didn't want to miss our opportunity to be on national television, so we went ahead with the performance.

We did our fire transfers seamlessly. Juggled with ease. All of that stuff was no problem. Our prop guy was waiting in the wings with a wet towel, as usual, just in case. It's funny, there was always a guy with a wet towel, but I had never seen him use it. He was just there all the time, with this dripping towel in case something went down, which it never did.

It was time for the grand finale, called The Human Volcano. We used highly flammable Coleman fuel in this act. To minimize our risk, we waited for the wind to change direction. As soon as we got a backwind, we took advantage of it. We couldn't speak to one another (because our mouths were full of Coleman fuel), so we communicated with hand signals.

1...2...3! We sprayed our fuel mist as hard as we could onto the torch. And we had extra fuel in our mouths for more effect.

WHOOSH!

The wind shifted right as we blew the Coleman fuel on the torch. The first guy was safe. The second guy had a little fuel spray on his face, which did not ignite.

My head and face were immediately engulfed in flame.

I heard the screaming in the stands before I felt anything. It was loud and frightening and seemed to never end.

Then I got tackled with a wet towel, and it was pressed over my face. I was whisked away behind the stage curtain. My dad came running toward me and yelled, "Let's get to the ER!" I'll never forget his face and the weird way he was looking at me. That's about when I started to think I might be in trouble. That's also about when the pain hit.

The head of the circus, Guppo—who was dressed in a clown suit and leading the band—also had a very odd look on his face as he watched me move along to the back. It's unsettling to see a man in a clown suit with his eyes popping out of his head.

My dad got me to the ER quickly. It was busy that day, so I had to wait in the ER in my sleek black fire costume with sequins and flames. I was the burnt fire guy.

It was starting to really hurt. I had third-degree burns, skin peeling off my face in a few different spots, and it was getting very unpleasant.

And the whole time, this guy's smiling at me. His daughter has a pretty gruesome splinter in her finger, and she is in pain, and he's smiling at me.

Michael: "What, dude? Why are you looking at me?"

Guy: "Well...you're the fire guy. And you caught fire."

Michael: "Uh...yeah."

Guy: "Did they get it on film?"

Michael: "Yeah, they did!"

To add insult to injury, my nurse was hot. I was fifteen and I had to drop my pants so she could give me a shot. I didn't think it could get any worse than that.

It did.

The doctor gave me a silver oxide cream to help heal the burns. I had to apply it to my face for three weeks. It was thick and white and looked like cheap clown makeup. And this was the very first three weeks of high school. Basically the worst time possible for this to happen.

I got teased at school. The kids asked me, "Hey Browne, what's up with the makeup?" However, I had a great answer: "I was eating fire on TV. What did you do last weekend?"

Of course, girls didn't find it all that attractive.

Our fire act never aired on *That's Incredible!*. Three of my good friends in the movie and entertainment industry are still searching for the footage today. If you find it, I have some really nice bottles of wine I'll trade you for it. Please look.

* * *

During our summer travels, we set up our circus at county fairs. We had a designated area, usually near a carnival. Obviously, we saw a lot of carnies. Young, immature, and bored, we would always mess with them. We'd start by scouting them out during the day. We wanted to find the best ones to harass. We stayed away from the ones who looked smart, or who had all their teeth. We focused on the ones who looked like they weren't quite as bright.

Once everyone went to bed, we would sneak over to the carny trailers, and all at once, just start pelting them with rocks. It was like a full-on assault. They would come running out screaming and yelling, and we'd run off laughing, go hide, wait for them to go back inside, then pelt their trailer again.

It was a lot of fun. Except this one night.

We did the standard recon, but I guess we messed it up because we hit the wrong trailer. Out came the carny brigade of half dressed, one-toothed wonders running out of their trailers. They were like the Walking Dead. I don't if they were methed up or drunk or what, but they weren't OK with just yelling at us. They woke up all the other carnies, and they came after us.

We hid in the bushes, held our breath, and didn't make a peep. None of us moved a muscle until they gave up the search. It's funny to think about now, but man, I was scared at the time. Carnies don't tend to be the most upstanding citizens, and these dudes were angry.

* * *

All the fun and games aside, the circus was maybe the most important part of my pre adult life. I firmly believe that the six years I spent in the circus is what led me to the success I've had in life, especially in wine.

For example, the circus taught me showmanship. It wasn't just enough to learn how to ride a unicycle, or learn how to do the trapeze. You had to do it with a certain flair, a certain style. You had to hold yourself up straight, you had to take a bow, you had to act gracious. Doing it right wasn't enough: you had to also *look like* you were doing it right, and then give the crowd the right cues and the space to recognize it. That's showmanship.

The circus taught me another crucial business lesson: respecting the audience. The circus is not about you; it's about your performance for the audience. You always go out and perform the best you can because people are paying to see you perform. You have to respect that—if you don't, then soon enough there won't be an audience. You need to make sure your costume is dialed in; you have to make sure that you do the best you can do. The audience deserves the respect of getting your best; they paid for that, after all. Even though I got to be one of the main players of the circus eventually, I never forgot that I was only in this position because people came to see us perform. That was my product and service, and I needed to give it my all to make sure they got what they paid for.

And man, the circus really taught me how to practice. I started as a gopher, and practiced to get on the unicycle team. Then I learned how to become a fire-breather. Then I worked really hard and got on the high-wire act (among other acts). Then I worked even harder and got on the trapeze act, the biggest one. And every step was incredibly hard work, full of mistakes and screwups.

But in the circus, that's cool. Screwing up is OK; it's how you learn. If something goes wrong, you do it again. Just don't give up. Do it again. When you fall off, get back on. If you mess up, do things over again. And do it even better the second time. The only way to really screw up was to stop trying.

I didn't realize I was learning this as I was learning it. All I cared about was getting on the next circus act. But man, going through all that failing and realizing it was OK—as long as I learned and kept going—was so crucial for me once I got into wine.

If there is one thing I learned more than any other from the circus, it was how to perform under pressure. How to deliver when people were relying on you.

There is one specific example of this that I still think about: the first time I rode the bicycle on the high-wire.

I practiced a lot, but every time I did, the wire was close to the ground. I didn't attempt to ride on the high-wire until just before my first performance. I knew how to ride a bicycle on the wire and had walked the high-wire before, and I practiced close to the ground; I didn't think it would be that hard to just combine everything.

The first time I got on the bicycle actually up on the high-wire was, like, two hours before showtime. For the first time, I'm twenty-five feet in the air on a bicycle. Only the front tire was on the wire. The back wheel was still on the platform.

I froze. I sat there on the bike, unable to move. I was legitimately scared.

So I re-centered myself and went through the steps.

First, I focused on the wire. I stared at that thing and nothing else.

Then, I started talking to myself.

I started with the worst-case scenario: "All right, if it doesn't work, if I freak out, I'll be OK. I know how to fall. If I do, I'm chucking everything—the pole, the bike—and I'm just gonna try to go straight down in the middle of the net."

That calmed me down. Then I started getting positive: "There's a show coming in two hours, and I'm committed to being the bike guy. I know I can do it. I told everybody I'd do it. There's nobody else prepped to do it, and it's a cool part of the act and I know how to do it. I just gotta get over this. I just gotta do it."

It took me fifteen minutes of doing this before I finally got past it.

Then when it came time for the actual show a few hours later, I was fine. I nailed it.

I cannot overstate how important this period was to my life and my success. When I feel like giving up on a goal or task, I think about this exact moment on the bicycle. Or I remind myself that it took a year of practice to conquer the fly bar. When the temptation to throw in the towel overtakes me, I remind myself of the fear I felt before riding on the high-wire. I overcame that fear.

All of these circus lessons: hard work, perseverance, giving my all, practice, second chances, and showmanship, helped shape who I am today.

It's not an accident that I named my new wine brand Cirq.

The circus is part of what made me who I am today.

CHAPTER 4

L.A.

MY FRIEND GLENN WAS THREE YEARS OLDER THAN ME. He was a talented drummer and aspired to be in a rock band. Glenn's dream of being in a rock band led him to move to L.A. I had initially planned on being in a professional circus in Australia after high school, but that fell through, so I went with him.

In 1987, we moved into a studio apartment. We were on the east side of town, at the end of Melrose Avenue. It wasn't like the TV show at all. It was cheap and ratty and rundown, but it was all we could afford, and hey—we were in L.A.

Glenn got me a job at Guitar Center in Hollywood. He worked in the drum department, and I sat at the front desk. I checked receipts, and I kicked bums, crazies, and prostitutes out of the store. This was on the Sunset Strip. Very different world than the apple town I grew up in.

The Nelson twins used to hang out there because their guitar player was an employee. One twin never gave me the time of day. The other twin was cool and down to earth. He sat with me at my desk when he waited for his friend, and we would talk. We had some cool, laid-back conversations.

Once, an older, chubby guy with a huge mustache came in to get equipment. He started chatting me up—he wanted to know my story. We talked for about forty-five minutes. He left, and the guitar tech asked me what we were talking about. I told him it was just random conversation. He told me I had been talking to David Crosby. I said, "Who's David Crosby?"

Other famous musicians came into the store. Two in particular stand out in my memory: Prince and Stevie Wonder.

Prince came into the store after we closed so he could have privacy. Bodyguards surrounded him. Prince didn't like it when people looked him in the eyes, so we were instructed to avoid eye contact.

No, seriously, the store manager explicitly told us to not look him in the eyes.

What the hell, man? I lost respect for him that day.

Another time, we found out someone famous would be visiting the store. The drill was the same—he would be coming in after close, so we had to stay and let him and his crew in.

Three Mercedes pulled up. The celebrity and his entourage got out of their cars, I unlocked the door for them and then locked the door behind them. I was used to this by now.

A guy I recognized was surrounded by at least ten body-guards. He was wearing sunglasses, and as he passed me on the way in, he looked at me and said, "Hey, how you doing?"

It was Stevie Wonder. He's blind.

A blind celebrity looked me in the eyes and spoke to me. He was very genuine, and I could tell he had respect for people. There was a sense of humility in him.

Prince, on the other hand, was a different story. Cool to see him, though. Quite a presence.

What these experiences taught me was that successful people are not unattainable gods who exist beyond the realm of men. They're just normal people doing their thing, right? At least most of them. Some had a pretty big opinion of themselves, which I guess I understand.

I know it sounds basic, but for a kid from the apple orchards of Washington, it was eye-opening. To see that successful people are not above anyone else, that they are regular people, doing their thing, earning a living, and that I can even do some of the things they do...it was important to me. I saw this some when I was doing flambés at the Thunderbird, but it was different in L.A.

This was a big-time experience for me, and I could find a place in this realm of successful people, even if it was small.

I could belong.

CHAPTER 5

FINDING WINE

I LEFT L.A. I LIKED IT, BUT IT WASN'T FOR ME. I WASN'T ready for the big time yet.

I wasn't sure what I wanted to do, but I knew I didn't want to do the professional circus in Australia. I was kind of over it.

I knew I wanted to go to school, but I didn't want to live in Wenatchee. I was kind of burned out on the place. I wanted to get out of Dodge, have a profession, and make money. I didn't want to make thirty grand per year for the rest of my life and retire at sixty-five. That wasn't for me—I would go crazy.

I had gotten into drafting in high school because I love to draw. I wanted to be an architect because you design a building however you want to design it, somebody builds it, and it's there forever. I thought that was cool.

Then you do something else, and you can be creative; it's your own style. I'd check out all the Frank Lloyd Wright buildings, stuff like that. Then, I thought, "Cal Poly in San Luis Obispo has a great architecture program. My grandparents live in Santa Rosa, so I'll go live with them to get my residency in California so I can afford tuition, and do that."

So, I went to live with my grandparents for a while. Since I had experience in fine dining, I got a job at Equus Restaurant at Fountaingrove Inn in Santa Rosa.

SANTA ROSA

I was nineteen then, and I was an assistant waiter at Equus. Then, I became a waiter. This was the hottest place in town at the time. It was old-school, man. We had Caesar salads done tableside, steak Diane, cherries jubilee, all that stuff. I was making bank and learning a lot.

I went to Santa Rosa Junior College. I was paying for it myself. I had to get my prerequisites before I could go to Cal Poly. Then, I could become an architect and live happily ever after. That was the goal.

I was into that process, but it was the same thing as high

school. I'd rather go hang with my buddies after my shift at the restaurant than go do homework. So, it took me four years to get my two-year degree, but I got it. It was a business associate's degree.

Before I got my associate's degree, I realized I didn't want to be an architect because calculus didn't make any sense to me. So, I decided to just figure things out from there. Let life be what it was going to be.

I remember the day I got my final credit for my associate's degree. I was supposed to sign something and get my paperwork and diploma...I just left. I was out of there. I did the work for the degree, and a piece of paper and diploma wasn't going to mean anything to me.

So, I left, and kept working at restaurants. I wanted to be a chef. I wanted to start cooking, because that's a craft, and I knew the restaurant business. I didn't want to have a tiny restaurant my whole life. I wanted to build a concept and a team, then build another concept and a team, and keep going. I wanted to follow the model of the company Real Restaurants.

I almost went to culinary school in New York, at the Culinary Institute of America, but I didn't want to bite that bullet financially. I decided I wanted to have a family, and if I did the restaurant gig, I would never see them. It wouldn't work.

HOW I FOUND WINE

I started getting into wine when I was about twenty. I was still working at the restaurant. The other waiters and I would all get the same day off and hit all these tasting rooms. It was like a cannonball run, you know?

Napa, Dry Creek, you name it. We'd just hit them on our days off and check these places out. It was cool because I grew up around agriculture—you go to these vineyards, and I would see that this is high-end agriculture. It's very precise.

Then, I'd go into some cool winery, and think, "Oh, man. There's a vibe going on here."

I was really into Silver Oak wine in '89, which was pretty early into Napa's modern wine business. Silver Oak was just starting to crank it up. At that point, they had some smoking wines. There was something about them.

So we decided to visit their winery one day, and it completely changed my life. It was the turning point that led me to where I am today.

When you go to Silver Oak in Napa, you go down a crossroad and then down a long driveway. I saw the vines, and I thought, "There's something here. I've been to a bunch of wineries, but there's something about this place."

I literally got out of the car and walked really close up to the vines. I looked at them and thought, "What the hell?" It was very cool, and it made sense to me. On a deep level, it all made sense.

I started the tour and there were all these old bottles to the right, and it smelled like oak and wine. They led me back to their little production area, where they have all this cool stainless-steel equipment. They took the fruit and processed it there, so it was kind of like food, but in a manufacturing sense. I'm a maker and craftsman, so this appealed to me.

Then, I walked into the barrel room. It was like a room full of angels, man. The energy. It was full of life. All the barrels were like individual energy pods. They were alive. That's how I felt about it, that's what I got from it. I feel the same today. The barrel room was magical to me then, and it still is.

At that point, they had the barrels on these wood beams and racks. I walked in there and felt like there was something living at rest in there. That's what it is, really. I felt that, but I didn't know what it was at the time.

I asked a tour guide if I could just walk around, and she told me to go for it. So, I started walking around. I'm touching the barrels and thinking, "What kind of energy is this?"

Then we started tasting barrels. I started getting into barrel tasting at different wineries and I saw the differences, and I saw this life and energy with the wine? It came from the earth, and it started making sense to me on a core level.

It was like walking into a room full of angels, except they were real. Or like a stable of horses looking at you, saying, "It's OK. We are so good right here." I patted the bottom of the barrels like the belly of a horse. I patted and rubbed them. I still do. Call me crazy, but I love to do that.

And when you think about it, the wine is literally alive in those barrels. Maybe I was just telling myself a story, but at that moment, I really felt like I could feel the life energy come off those barrels and "speak" to me, in a sense.

They don't speak to you in a sense that they really "talk" to you, but they put out some kind of energy. And it's different with each barrel. It's totally bizarre, and I don't know if I am explaining this well. I've talked about this with other wine people and some get it, while some look at me like I'm nuts.

I just know I felt this right away. When I walked into that room, I think it was the first barrel room I had ever walked into. There was a deep, textured energy—a feeling. For some reason, it just made sense to me. I think with all of the other experiences I'd had with agriculture, food, and finished products, and the surroundings, I just connected with it.

So, anyway, that's what it felt like. It's simplistic, but it was very deep, meaningful, and complex.

At that moment, I knew. I knew I wanted to be a winemaker. I knew this was my path in life.

I think what I loved about it was that it encompassed different aspects of craftsmanship and business that I was good at and liked. I could go make cabinets, but cabinet shops are like many other crafts: hard to make a living at. I love high-end woodwork, but I didn't know about the shops, and that wasn't interesting to me.

Money wasn't important per se, but I wanted to be successful. I wanted to have a conduit, a business that could actually make enough money to not worry about money. With the wines and these amazing estates, I thought, "Wow. They've got to be making money here."

Most importantly, I wanted to encompass craftsmanship and the agriculture that I loved. I grew up sitting in cherry trees and eating fruit. I knew how to grow things and how to make things, and this was the perfect combination of the two.

At the wine production facility, they had all this cool equipment and neat stuff, and it was all in order. It was clean, glistening, and ready for business. The barrel room brought it all together—it was an all-encompassing thought about the wine. Then the business side of my brain started latching on to it.

That day at Silver Oak planted the seed.

But how would I do that? I had no idea.

I thought I had to have a degree. You look at all of these different jobs, and you need a degree. I thought it was going to take me twelve to fifteen years to get there. I thought I would have to go to school, then be an intern, and I would be thirty-five before I could get going. Mainly because I am a terrible student in the classic form of school and in my mind at that time, it would take me that long before I could get a degree. I didn't want to do that. Not that I did not want to work hard—I did. I just wanted to find a different path. School of hard knocks, so to speak.

I decided I would find another way. I had no idea how, but I would.

THE DREAM OF MAKING WINE

Soon after, I got a job at John Ash & Co. restaurant in Santa Rosa, which at the time was probably the very best restaurant in the area and still remains up there to this day. I worked there for ten years as a waiter, manager, bartender, lead grill cook, pastry chef, and sommelier.

John Ash had super high-end food, stuff I'd never seen before. It was cool then, and it's still cool now. That's where I got exposed to high-end food and all the high-end wine. At the same time, we were going out to wineries all over the place. I realized some of them were great, and some of the wines I really dug—some were magical, for some reason. They just grabbed me. Different wineries will grab different people.

Then, I started exploring, and people would tell me to talk to this guy and that guy, or go to a certain dinner and meet with this guy, etc. Once, I went to a Ravenswood winemaker dinner and I sat next to Joel Peterson, a co-founder of Ravenswood. This was in '94. I kept asking him questions, and he started telling me about toasting and sourcing of barrels, and all these things I didn't know at all. I had never talked to anyone about barrels. It was an hour-and-a-half-long conversation, and we could have talked for five hours.

He's talking about toasting and sourcing, and I said, "I had no idea."

He said, "Oh yeah, man. There's a lot going on."

Think about this—wine barrels are utterly crucial to wine

making, yet I had never even considered that aspect, nor had anyone even talked to me about it.

It opened my eyes to the fact that I had to meet as many experienced wine people as I could and ask them questions to learn directly from them. It was fascinating—like another world. And this was a world that was deep and infinitely complex and would keep me interested for the rest of my life.

After that, I met Daryl Groom, who previously was the lead winemaker at Penfolds in Australia and then at Geyser Peak in Sonoma County.

I said to Daryl, "I'm not sure if I want to settle here or settle back in Washington State. This whole wine thing, I don't want to go to school for twelve years. I'm going to hit dead ends. I don't want to be an intern for ten years after ten years of school."

He told me not to go to school. He said to start my internship right now, with someone making wine. He told me that winemakers were really cool people and they would help me if I was sincere and hardworking.

In the meantime, I met this guy, Robert Rex, at Deerfield Ranch. I went out with him to help pick grapes and make wine at his little winery. So, I had a connection there. I could have gotten a job at bigger wineries as an intern, but that's not what I wanted. I wanted to work with someone who had their hands in all aspects of wine and understood the full craft, as well as the business side.

I ended up going back to Washington State to see if I wanted to settle there. I got a job at a couple of restaurants while I was up there. Lampreia in Seattle was killer. This guy, Scott Carsberg, was there as chef owner. He crafted incredible food and designed an exceptional restaurant experience. Very well tuned in. To this day I am still blown away by what he did.

I worked there and at another restaurant, but I wanted to be in the wine business. One of my bosses at the other restaurant told me to go to a certain wine distributor because they were the best one. I got a job selling wine for them pretty quickly. I had one of the best routes in Seattle: Ballard and Fremont, that whole area. I was selling big wines, like Beringer, Mondavi, Kendall-Jackson, and other stuff. I was a wine rep for one of the distributors called Western Washington Beverage. They're gone now.

I gotta be honest: I hated it. Very cool company, but just not for me in any sense.

I was selling all these wines that the distributor treated like commodities during the sales process. All these wines were and are very good wines, but I hated how I had to sell them. It was not for me.

I was still in touch with Robert Rex at Deerfield Ranch, and he offered me an internship. Said it was available if I wanted it, but he couldn't pay me. That was fine with me. I wasn't looking for a paycheck; I was looking for experience.

I thought about it a lot. And I finally made the decision to go back.

At the time I was dating a great girl named Sarah. When I told her I was unhappy and had to make a change, she thought I was breaking up with her.

"No, no. I'm going to move back to Sonoma County and volunteer at this winery, Deerfield Ranch."

I could have gotten jobs at bigger wineries, but I wanted to do small because I would actually be making the wine. Deerfield wouldn't be paying me, but the important thing was that I would be in the middle of it all. I told her that I thought I could get my job back at John Ash. I could sleep on my best friend, Steve's, futon.

I asked her if she wanted to go.

Sarah: "What?"

Michael: "I know, I didn't think I would ask that either. But I want you to come."

It wasn't a well-thought-out plan. I was a noncommittal dude. I'd have a girlfriend for a while, but I was not the type to make a commitment; it took me by surprise that I asked her. But it's what I felt.

I wanted to be with a good, real person who would be a good mother. I had blown a couple of those opportunities already. Then I met Sarah, who was the best woman I'd ever met, and I told myself I wasn't going to blow this one. I had thought about her coming with me, but it wasn't like me to ask a girl something like that.

I really liked her family. Her aunt put me up against the wall and said, "If you mess with her, I'm going to mess with you," that sort of thing. It didn't scare me off; I thought it was cool, actually. These people took life seriously. More than that, they took family seriously, something very important to me.

In the end, she looked at me and said, "OK. I'll come with you."

She moved down, and I volunteered at Deerfield, got my job back at John Ash, and set up camp on my buddy's futon.

It was really hard at first. She was working days, and I was working nights. It was harvest time, and we weren't seeing each other much. It was a new relationship, and she was out of her element.

Sarah: "I don't know about this. I never see you, and I don't know what's going on."

Michael: "It will be cool. Someday we'll have our own winery. Believe me. We're going to have it. I know it. Don't worry; it's going to work out. We'll live in a little bungalow in the hills, and I'll make enough to cover our family's expenses. We'll eat good food, see good friends, and call it a day."

There was no evidence that this was going to happen; I just felt it.

I wish I could tell you there was some secret to it or I had some trick. There wasn't. I just knew I could be successful when I found out what I wanted to do, and once I realized it was wine, I just decided I was going to make it work.

I told myself I would give this wine endeavor ten years, and if it didn't work out, the worst thing that would happen is that I learned how to make wine, I met a bunch of great people, and I spent ten years living in the Garden of Eden.

LEARNING WINE

My clearest memory at Deerfield was in 1997. That was when I made my first vintage wine.

Deerfield was interesting because I really liked the owner and winemaker there, Robert Rex. He was kind of a Renaissance man. He had a lot of interests, and wine was one of them. It was his favorite interest. He loved being in the vineyards and winery but had many other duties running the business with his wife, PJ, and he needed help. I wanted to help and learn.

The problem is that I didn't know *how* to do any of it.

For example, how do you clean a barrel? There is an art and skill to it, and I had no idea how to do it, nor did anyone teach me the complexities of the process. Robert basically said, "Here's a barrel, here's a hose and a barrel-washer, here's how you do it."

I had no idea how complex that simple task could be.

At that time, I would have liked a different way of doing things, but I wouldn't change the experience. I learned from my mistakes and that was very valuable. I had no preconceived ideas. I learned how to use the equipment through trial and error. And I even ended up coming up with certain techniques through trial and error, many of which I still use to this day. I think figuring out how to do things, or at least trying, was one of the keys to my success.

Let's stick with washing a barrel to explain why this "trial and error" method was so valuable. Washing a barrel is very important. We didn't have the right equipment—the best equipment to wash a barrel. We didn't have the best hot water situation either. I didn't know how to gas a barrel properly, or how to hold back the microbes, etc. How do you swell a barrel up, pound hoops, and plug the holes from the bore beetles? I just went for it and kept trying things until I got it right.

Every aspect of making wine is a craft, even the barrel cleaning. When you take the wine out of the barrels, there are some solids in there, and they kind of stick. There are also tartrates.

When you take wine out of the barrel, you want to clean the barrel. If the barrel is going to be empty, you have to clean it well, because you're going to use it again. You won't use a barrel forever, but you need to have it properly sanitized. If you don't, it will grow mold and other microbes that are detrimental to the process.

For example, imagine it's your last turn on a barrel. You're getting ready to store it for three or four months before you fill it up or use it again. You take the wine out, and there are some lees left in it—it looks like really thick Pepto-Bismol. The lees are the solids, consisting of yeast cells and bacteria.

The solids are from the grapes—just matter that settles out. Then, you get tartrate buildup if the cellar is cold. The wine will precipitate tartrates and they become crystals. If you've ever seen a cork with crystals on it—those are tartrates. They're difficult to remove, and they will form inside of some barrels. You want to clean those off. You can sanitize them, but it's very porous. Stuff can more readily grow within that environment if solids are still in there. There's more surface area for things to grow on.

We use a high-pressure barrel wand with hot water. It's not boiling water, but it's pretty hot, like 120 to 140 degrees. The nozzle turns back and forth. It shoots high, too—you can shoot water thirty feet into the air. It gets rid of all the junk. We didn't have that at Deerfield.

We had a little wand with a spinner that was like a sprinkler. It's not the best tool, but a lot of people use them. It just doesn't do an effective job. You can clean with it, but you aren't done. You still have to rinse it out. Thankfully, not too soon after I started, Robert got a really nice barrel cleaner. Great tool to have.

At Deerfield, we had to do it until it ran clear. You use a lot of water, and it has to be hot water—as hot as you can get it. So, eventually it works, it's just a huge pain in the ass. It doesn't work as well as the good equipment, but you can get it to work.

Now, we use steam in our barrels, which is very effective. It's a better method and does a better job. Then you let them dry upside down for a day. Next, you turn them right-side up, and you put sulfur gas in them. You put a little Dixie cup in the bunghole because you want it to breathe a little bit, but not be totally open.

You put the Dixie cup in there, and then you tilt them on their side a little bit—one o'clock, two o'clock. You let them sit, and then once a month you go back and rinse them again. You don't go through the entire process again because they are clean, but you do want to rinse and re-gas them.

It's a once-a-month process. It's not overkill, but it's very labor-intensive. That's how we do it now. Now, not only do I know how to wash a barrel, I know how NOT to wash a barrel as well. I can step into any part of the barrel washing process and know exactly what's going on, to this day. All because I ruined a lot of barrels and learned what not to do and then learned the proper method of barrel sanitization.

Barrel cleaning is just one aspect of wine making, and it is crucial. Now imagine this sort of attention to detail for everything else—farming and picking grapes, fermentation, blending and bottling, just to name a few. This is why Deerfield was so great for me, and why I wanted to learn hands-on.

MORE MISTAKES

I made a lot of mistakes in my early career, especially when I was making wine for three different wineries at once. I can remember one time that was especially bad.

It started during the bottling process that specific year. Bottling is always the hardest thing because that's when all your hard work from farming, fermentation, barrel aging, and blending culminates in bottling, and you can mess it up so easily at that point if you aren't careful.

One time I was by myself, racking the wines, cleaning the barrels, blending, getting the wine bottle-ready, and making sure we had all the supplies set up. I was up until five in the morning and it was an insane, mind-blowing amount of work. For this run, there was one person, me, doing the entire preparation for the bottling process. Six thousand cases of wine. Five different wines.

To help you understand how much work this was, if I were to make that much wine today, I'd have a minimum of six people doing it, including myself.

I had it dialed in and I knew how to do it, but it was like eighteen to nineteen hours each day to get it done. I'd leave at 2:00 a.m., get four hours of sleep, and be back before the sun was up.

I laid out all the barrels and got to work. I racked all the barrels, turned them upside down, and got all the lees out of them. I didn't have time to wash them, so I turned them right-side up and put a bung in them. There was still lees residue inside; I stacked them up to get to them later. I put a little sulfur in them.

There were other people there who were being paid to help, but they were too busy to help, because this was a custom crush facility with many producers under one roof.

Then, I had to rack the wines by myself. Very time-consuming because you have to get it right, and you can only go so fast. You have to make sure the blends are all accurate and blended properly. You have to stir the tank, run the samples to the lab, make sure the chemistry is correct in all aspects, all the while ensuring that everything is gassed properly using inert gas to keep oxygen away from the wine, to get it all bottle-ready.

Then, on bottling day at 5:00 a.m., the bottling trucks showed up. This time we didn't have our capsules on time. The bottling crew was there, but all they do is run the bottling truck, so I had to get all the hoses sanitized and over to the truck, solo. That's a big job in itself. Right now, we have a crew of seven temps and six full-time people doing this stuff. You could get it done with four people, but we have more working so we can monitor quality control and all these other details.

I was hauling ass, getting the hoses to the truck to start bottling at 7:00 a.m., but I was also still racking wines that need to be bottled later that day, so I was on a timeline that seemed impossible.

I had a two-thousand-pound canister of argon to charge and pressurize the barrels; it pushes the wine through a device and into the tank. To change out the tanks, I had to go to one side of the building, grab them, pull them back, take the regulator off, put a new regulator on, turn a bunch of valves, turn it up and on, and then start over again. I got to the last two barrels, and the argon tank started to run out.

I thought I could get the last two barrels out of it, so I had the regulator all the way open. It stopped. Great, I've got to get a new canister for the very end. So I ran and got a canister, had the valve closed on the barrel, from the barrel to the tank. There was nowhere for the wine to go if the barrel was pressurized.

You have to have the valve turned off to make sure you don't leak. So I hooked the regulator up to the new argon tank. The regulator should have been turned off. But instead I left the regulator completely open, and forgot.

This is not good. It was two thousand pounds of pressure coming from the regulator, and it was fully open with the valve to the wine tank closed. Nowhere for the wine to go.

I heard a sound I'd never heard before. It was the barrel getting ready to burst under the pressure.

It blew the head of the barrel completely off. It was one of the best barrels of the lot. Boom. The wine went everywhere. It went straight down the drain. It emptied in two seconds. Gone.

About four hours later, I did it again, on a different lot. I wasted two barrels, about fifty cases of wine. It was a few thousand bucks down the drain. All because I was way too busy and tired, but I had no choice.

Another time, I was at Deerfield because we made our Kosta Browne wine there for a couple of years, getting ready to bottle the '05 vintage. I was finishing the Russian River lot, which was bottle-ready, and I was all by myself at midnight. I had to stir the tank, but at that point, we didn't have a proper stirrer. We have a cool mixer now, but we couldn't afford it at that point.

I got all the wine into the tank. It was all set, and the wine tasted cool and groovy. I just wanted to mix it for thirty minutes or so, while I was cleaning up, because I had a big cleanup job on my hands. I hooked up this pump that had two valves on the inlet, and two valves on the outlet. I would valve them off, switch hoses, then open valves to reverse the flow and properly stir the tank. They were two-inch hoses, and one was through the top of the tank, which was basically a very large siphon, about twenty feet tall. I had the hose at the top secured so it would not fly out.

I was sitting there thinking, "OK, it's time to change it." I closed the valves and took the clamp off the hose. There are fittings called tri clovers, and there's a gasket in the middle of it. You put them together, you put a clamp around it, and it's tight. It doesn't leak. Then, I got these valves, so I could close both valves and take the middle clamp off. So it's two clamps, two valves, two clamps. I was going to take these off, switch them, put them back on, open it back up, turn it the other way, and finish blending the tank.

Twenty minutes, then I could be done with the hoses and go to sleep. All right, it's time to change it. I got down there, and I decided which one to take off first. I closed all the valves. Instead of taking the valve off, I took the hose off, which was siphoned to the top of the tank.

Suddenly, a fire hose of wine was spraying out all over the place, and I was by myself.

The hose was bungee-corded so tight I couldn't pull it out of the top of the wine. It was probably five feet into the wine, six or seven barrels worth, or something: a lot of money, dude. Translate that into direct-to-consumer sales, and it was tens of thousands of dollars.

What could I do? I couldn't take the wine hose up the ladder, and I had this jet engine I was trying to carry around with me. Wine's flying everywhere, and as I looked down at the floor—I saw a gasket.

So I grabbed the clamp and put it in my mouth. I grabbed the gasket, put it on, and held it. The wine started spraying all in my face. I swear my eyelids flipped back and I couldn't see anything.

I was trying to put the hose back on the valve, but it was going up against immense force. I don't know how many pounds of pressure it was, but the wine was squirting ten feet around me. It was a fire hose of wine. It was spraying in my face. I was covered in wine; my eyelids were flipping back. I lost my contacts.

I finally had a chance to get it on there on the second or third attempt. I took it, and I had to get this in with one hand. Wham! I got it on. Whew.

I lost at least two barrels, and that was a big financial loss for us.

Anyway, I cleaned it up, got it done, came back at five in the morning for bottling, and this wine got number seven in the world from *Wine Spectator*. Imagine that.

Learning wine is not easy.

CHAPTER 6

THE KOSTA
BROWNE STORY

THE BEGINNING

I MET DAN KOSTA AT JOHN ASH & CO. IN 1992. WE BOTH
left that place numerous times, and they always took us back.
Dan was mainly the restaurant manager and the wine buyer.
I was touring the restaurant, doing different things all the
time and learning the restaurant business. At that time I
was really interested in opening my own restaurant company,
and I was into learning every aspect of the business, and
John Ash was the place.

When I moved back down from Seattle in 1997, I went to
John Ash and Dan was managing at the time. I needed a job,
and I really liked the place and I knew what to do. It was
only a matter of if he had a position available.

Dan: "Sure, love to have you back. What are you doing back in town?"

Michael: "I decided to come back to make wine."

Dan: "Oh, you're going to make wine? I've been thinking about doing the same thing."

I always liked Dan, and I always thought he'd make a good business partner at something, but I didn't know he wanted to make wine. So we decided that every night that we worked together, we'd save ten dollars of our tip money each and put it in an envelope. Once we saved enough money to buy some grapes, we'd make wine. If we could get a half ton, that's enough to make a barrel of wine, plus topping wine.

The issue was that this was June, and we had limited time until harvest, and we had no money at the time. We saved our money, and soon we had almost enough for a half ton of grapes. We talked to the chef at that time, Jeffrey Madura, and he said he'd give us the rest of the money we needed and then we could split the wine a third each.

We also bought a hand crank destemmer from the local fermentation joint. We got grapes from some random dude, a guy who knew the owner of the vineyard. The vineyard was somewhere on Eastside Road, but we never visited the site because we couldn't find it.

I think the owner had a field of grapes and told our guy, "Sometimes you can get three tons an acre, sometimes four. It varies." The guy probably just peeled some off, didn't tell the owner, and sold it to us. I'm not sure, but the way he sold the grapes to us, it didn't feel all that legit. I didn't know what Pinot Noir looked like at the time; I was just going on his word, assuming it was all Pinot Noir.

We bought these grapes, we bought a barrel, had a destemmer, and Robert Rex allowed us to make it at his small home at Deerfield. It was great to be able to make the wine with some of the tools we needed, rather than trying to get it out of our bathtub or something like that.

We got the grapes, picked them up at a random winery, brought them back to Deerfield, and started putting them through the hand crank destemmer. About a third of the way through, we noticed the grapes looked different. They were bigger, more plump, lighter in color, and didn't taste right. Robert Rex was there and since he's been around a long time in the wine business, he said, "That's Gamay Beaujolais; that's not Pinot Noir."

We started sorting the grapes any way we could, which meant sifting through the bin by hand, and dumped the Gamay into the stem pile for mulch. We thought it was about 200 pounds.

We fermented the wine and took very good care of it. It

was our baby. Robert helped us along the way since we had no idea what we were doing. The fermentation was healthy and finished, which was a big deal (which I didn't know at the time). It's funny to think about now, how little we knew about wine and how lucky we got.

The wine came out tasting really good. We still have one bottle left in the cellar at Kosta Browne, and that's it from the first vintage. I don't think wine from that bottle will ever be tasted.

We also made a Late Harvest French Colombard, the same year, 1997. For that, we got the grapes for free. John Ash had a field next to the restaurant just to paint a pretty picture—they pruned everything to make it look good, but they didn't sell those grapes. The French Colombard vineyard was old, head-pruned, but still made some pretty good grapes, even though no one used them.

The grapes were starting to mold with botrytis, which was great for late harvest (think of Sauternes). We asked the owner if we could go out there and pick grapes. He said, "Knock yourself out."

So, we showed up there at seven in the morning on a Sunday. I was in my broken-down Jetta, and Dan seemed to be a bit hungover, which was a normal condition for us in those days. We got bus tubs and scissors out of the kitchen and we hit the field. It was an acre. I started at one end, Dan started at the other, and we planned to meet in the middle.

We clipped little grapes off each cluster, which had just the right amount of botrytis, and threw them in the tubs. Mold spores flew everywhere.

At one point, I looked up and Dan was gone. He was lying down in the vineyard, nursing some wounds and gaining strength for the rest of the day. I got him up, and we kept going.

We loaded the big tubs of grapes into my Jetta and went to his house on Strawberry Lane in Santa Rosa. It was starting to rain, and we rented a little basket press from The Beverage People. It was a wooden one that we had to hand crank. Mind you, we had no idea how to use this, much less how to press moldy grapes.

We loaded the grapes in, and it was a slimy mess. It was rotten grapes with mold spores, you know? We loaded the grapes into this thing, and we just tried to figure it out. We had a ratchet on it, and it just formed a mass—nothing came out. It was just a big chunk.

So we thought we had to stab it to loosen it up. We got a crowbar out. We started stabbing it with a crowbar we got from the garage. We moved it around, pressed it, released it, stabbed it, and this brownish-greenish slimy stuff started coming out of it. We nicknamed it frog sap, because it looked like the stuff that might come out of a frog if you squeezed it. We also coined the term "let's stab the cake" from that.

We were left with a bin of nasty juice, and I said, "OK, let's settle it, then ferment it. I'll get some yeast, and I think we can just ferment it, and then we'll take the next step."

After fermentation, I called Robert. He said, "You have to get some bentonite to get rid of the solids. It's clay. Things bind to it, and they settle out more heavily."

I didn't know I had to rehydrate it for a day or two—it makes a slurry but takes time to hydrate. The only thing we knew how to do was cook, so we put it on the stove and cooked it so it would dissolve. This was pretty idiotic, if you don't know. I had been working at Deerfield for one month at this point; I had no idea what I was doing.

We cooked it, added it to the wine, settled it out, and I went to Washington for the holidays. I called Dan, and he said he thought it was ready. I said, "Here's what you're gonna do. Go to The Beverage People; get some 375ml bottles and corks. Fill up all the bottles, use Private Preserve inert gas, and gas them. Then, seal them up."

He got it done. I think we had sixty bottles total. We brought it to the restaurant. The taste was killer. It was a dessert wine, really sweet and good. If we had some today, I believe it would still taste great.

So, we made the Pinot and this late harvest wine. Some cool people came in, and we asked them if they wanted to taste something we made (more on our philosophy on this is coming later). We poured the Pinot, they thought it was good, and we sold some wine—they took it right out the door. We sold it for twenty-five bucks a bottle, and one guy bought four cases.

We thought, "Cool, we're making our money back."

THE FIRST INVESTORS

The next year, we met two guys: a commodities broker and a Scotsman.

These guys would go out and party. I would take care of them at the bar at John Ash, and I told them what we were doing. They said they were interested in it, too, so I said, "Cool. Let's make a couple barrels of wine. I can get some Zinfandel, and we can pick Sauvignon Blanc right here." The vineyard behind the restaurant was Sauvignon Blanc land.

We bought grapes from the owner—a half ton of Sauvignon Blanc, and a half ton of Zinfandel from another grower through Deerfield. We made both, and both sucked. We got rid of the Zinfandel barrel and bottled the Sauvignon Blanc. It was house wine that we drank ourselves. Not easy to drink, but we did.

The reason we picked Sauvignon Blanc was because it was an up-and-coming varietal, and it was selling and we liked it, and the grapes were less expensive and faster to turn around. No barrels involved, and easier to move. Revenues came more quickly that way.

Then I said, "There's a good opportunity for Sauvignon Blanc. I know a vineyard up in Lake County; they want to sell us a field. Are you guys in?"

We raised three hundred thousand dollars from these two guys. We didn't sign any paperwork or anything; it was just a handshake agreement.

My paycheck was a truck. The investors couldn't afford to pay us, and they knew I was tired of driving the Jetta. So, they leased me a truck. I have fond memories of the Jetta, but I was glad to see it go.

We made our first commercial release of Kosta Browne in 1999. It was a Sauvignon Blanc. 3,650 cases of it. I thought it wasn't that much, and we could do it. Then, the trucks started showing up with grapes. Holy shit. We took on WAY more than what we should have.

Dan and I were up until five in the morning processing the stuff—I was just winging it. We used some skin contact, pressed it, and fermented it. Then, we bottled it. I had been at Deerfield for two years at this point.

OUR NAME AND OUR FIRST WINES

The wine we made turned out good. A *New York Times* article said it was the number one Sauvignon Blanc. We called it Kosta Browne.

We didn't start with Kosta Browne, though. The first dessert wine and Pinot didn't have a name. Then for the Sauvignon Blanc, the first name we chose was Alterra. Using my old architecture and creative skills, I drew a cluster with a pencil for the first label design. That is the cluster graphic on the Kosta Browne label.

Turns out that the name was already taken for wine. Some guy found out about the name because our partners were bar guys, and they talked to someone who talked to someone else. That guy called me and said, "That's my name, and you can't have it."

I thought, "Damn, we're two months from bottling, and the label is designed." Dan and I talked:

Me: "We're kind of modeling after Williams Selyem, so let's just call it our names."

Dan: "Is it Kosta Browne, or is it Browne Kosta?"

Me: "Well, Browne Kosta sounds like a disease you catch in Thailand, or a nasty spider. So, let's call it Kosta Browne."

So, that's how we came up with the name Kosta Browne.

There's a full six-liter of the '99 Kosta Browne Sauvignon Blanc still at John Ash. I printed the label for that bottle on an inkjet printer in my garage, twenty years ago. You can still tell it came off an inkjet printer if you look up close. I dosed it with one thousand parts sulfur. You usually put fifty parts in, but I put in one thousand. I didn't want it to oxidize and turn brown. And it worked: the wine has still not oxidized to this day.

But I wouldn't drink it, because with that much sulfur, it'll be terrible. And you might die. Or at least get a real bad headache.

THE SAUVIGNON BLANC GUYS

We made the 3,650 cases of '99 Sauvignon Blanc at Roche Winery (which is now the new Ram's Gate). We rented the space from them so we could do our own thing there. It was cool. We made wine there until 2002. We went from twenty-five cases, to fifty, to 3,650 in three years. We started making wine on a scale far beyond what we had done before.

Let me tell you: doing 3,650 cases of wine is insane. I already told you about the two trucks full of grapes that pulled up. They were big doubles. They were so big they didn't have grape bins; they had pear bins because Lake County was pear country. So, they brought these bigger bins with grape condoms (a grape condom is a big plastic sack in the bin so the juice won't leak out).

It's messy. You process it, and then you make the wine.

Fast forward to the bottling of our first commercial wine. A big semi pulled up with the bottles right before bottling. The first truck pulled up:

Michael: "Cool. Do I need to sign for this?"

Driver: "The last guy will have it."

Michael: "What do you mean, 'the last guy'?"

Driver: "There are three more trucks coming."

Michael: "Oh, damn."

It was a lot of glass. Dan was the sales and marketing dude. He helped me during a harvest, but I did everything else in terms of production. I was the only one at Roche making the wine for Kosta Browne (though I did get some help from John Farrington and Robert Rex along the way).

I kind of knew the process, and I half-ass knew the details. But let's be honest: I was lost a lot of the time. I can't tell you how many times I'd find myself on the phone with Robert, asking things like, "How long should I keep it on the skin? What should my pH be? And what do I add, and when?" Thank God he was there to help as well as John Farrington. I am forever grateful.

We had hiccups when it came to selling that Sauvignon Blanc too. How do you sell that much wine, when you're new guys with no experience? We decided to get a broker on the East Coast, Jack Lynch.

He's an old broker. He moved a bunch of wine for us. Then, we got some other distributors, and we made it through the 3,650 cases of wine.

We hit trade tastings. John Farrington told me that Williams Selyem used to hit every marketing event they could. They kept their brand out there, went to the tastings, all the stuff. So, I had these big nine-liters of Sauvignon Blanc. Why? Because nobody makes nine liters of Sauvignon Blanc.

People would come up to us at Family Winemakers, which

is a consumer tasting for wine. They'd ask, "What's this?" We'd say, "It's Sauvignon Blanc." "So, you're the Sauvignon Blanc guys?" "Yep, that's right."

We did that because it was quick turnaround, and quick revenues. We'd get into Pinot eventually when we had enough money to do that. That's what we really wanted to do, but it was too capital intensive at that time.

OVERCROPPED

The next year, 2000, we made Sauvignon Blanc and a bit of Pinot Noir, and they overcropped the Sauvignon Blanc in a big way. We wanted fifty tons, and there were something like 120 tons out there.

So what did I do? I got on the phone and sold grapes.

The problem was that the grapes didn't ripen up because there was too much fruit. I didn't know what to tell the vineyard manager, because I wasn't a grower. I didn't know what the hell I was doing in a vineyard. I went out there and there was fruit everywhere.

So, I was hustling grapes to other wineries that had a big Sauvignon Blanc program by the semi load. I was able to move quite a bit, although not as much as I would have liked. Last minute stuff. I couldn't press it at Roche because it was too much to handle. I had to take it somewhere up in Mendocino County.

I went in there, and they pressed it out. I said, "Can you do some quick numbers?" They did, and then they're telling me, "Dude, your fruit is eighteen brix. It's supposed to be something like twenty-two or twenty-three."

I said, "Oh, really?" Then they said, "Yeah, man. You picked a little early."

I messed up, man. I totally blew it. It didn't end up having much flavor. It sucked, and we had a LOT of it. We probably had 4,000 or 5,000 cases.

That same year we got some Pinot Noir through John Farrington, who used to work at William Selyem. It came from Cohn Vineyard, one of the oldest Pinot Noir vineyards in Sonoma County, a vineyard in which Williams Selyem had made a few vintages.

We split it between John Farrington, Deerfield, and ourselves. That was the first commercial Kosta Browne Pinot Noir. This was in 2000.

We did that, and we ended up with eight barrels of Pinot, plus 4,000 cases of Sauvignon Blanc that didn't taste good.

As a side note, the 2000 Kosta Browne is dedicated to John Farrington because in the summer of 2001, he unfortunately passed away. He was a dear friend and taught me a lot.

BREAKING UP WITH THE INVESTORS

At this point, we realized the investors hadn't been helping us beyond the money they gave us.

We got $300,000 from the investors. We had no ownership structure laid out—nothing. We didn't know what we were doing. At one point in the beginning, Dan said he didn't want investors. He said he was out; I told him I was going with the investors. A week later, he decided he was in. This whole Kosta Browne thing almost didn't happen.

I don't know what changed his mind, or if he had talked to someone, or whatever. I never asked. He probably realized we needed investors because we had no money. At the end of 2000, we realized they weren't paying the checks on time, but our names were on the label. It wasn't that they didn't want to, but this was a side project for them. This was our name on the bottle and our reputation. The partnership was not working out, so we needed to do something.

They had an LLC agreement with each other, and we weren't a part of it. We weren't part of the agreement, thank God.

We started thinking, "We don't have anything, and they are not paying the bills on time." They weren't bad guys; they just weren't grooving with our style and our state of mind as young, hungry entrepreneurs. We realized these guys weren't the best partners for us.

I pointed out to Dan that we had all the leverage. "We didn't sign anything. They need to finish this wine that's still in the tank. We could walk away from this tomorrow. We're not legally bound."

We sat down with the investors in a private room at Vineyards Inn, and we negotiated a split.

I said, "This isn't working. We need to split up the assets. So, if we can have the brand name, the Pinot Noir, and 800 cases of Sauvignon Blanc, you can have the rest of it; the bulk of the Sauvignon Blanc. I'll finish that wine for you, and you've got to come up with your own label idea."

They came up with a label and a design; I honestly can't even remember it. I got their share of the wine bottled for them. Then, we wanted to cut all ties. The investors tried to get more out of us, so we told them they could just have it all. We were walking. That was the type of leverage we had in the situation.

It got a little intense, but we were able to get what we

wanted in the end. A rough situation, but we needed to do what we needed to do.

Then, the Costellos came on board in 2001. Now it's Dan, Chris Costello, and me.

So we had the name, some Sauvignon Blanc in tank, some Pinot Noir in barrel, and obligations we had to get through—we had contracts with growers for more grapes. But no money.

A NEW BUSINESS PLAN

I wanted to come through and do this thing, but we had no money to do it. Dan's dad, Tom, knew a guy named Rick Markoff. He formerly worked for Xerox, and he was a sage in business.

He said, "Write a business plan, submit it, and if it makes sense, I'll submit it to this other guy. If it works, we'll proceed with some conversations." I was thankful for all the reading and studying of business plans I had done in the past—it took me two months to write it.

I got all of my business planning books out. The plan was a big, thick thing with graphs and pretty pictures. The word "great" was in there about 1,000 times. I had to create spreadsheets, but I didn't know how to sum a column in

Excel. I was too proud to ask for help, so I added everything up by calculator. Summing a column is one of the most basic functions in Excel. Not for me at the time, though.

I triple-checked my numbers. Insane. I went to Kinko's, got the plans bound up, and then I showed up at John Ash. Dan was just getting off his shift with his buddies, and I handed him the plan. "Here you go. Boom." Dan said, "Cool. All right." He looked through it that night and thought it was great.

Then, we gave a copy to Rick Markoff, and about a month later Rick said, "OK, let's meet at Café Mocha in Santa Rosa." We met with him, and he slammed it on the table, "Fellas, this is amateur crap. You won't raise a dollar with this. But, I'm gonna tell you how to redo it."

I was offended for about a minute, and then I thought, "Cool." This was a great opportunity to learn from a real pro.

We spent three hours together. He was crossing things out on every page, and asked, "Michael, what's up with all the 'greats' everywhere in this?" I had no good answer.

Rick says, "People aren't going to look at all the graphs. And you need to tighten up your spreadsheets. Tighten this stuff up with my notes, then come back with it." So, he helped us whittle it down to something that made sense. We wanted to raise a million dollars, and only do Pinot Noir.

Then Chris Costello took it and rewrote it based on Rick's comments and instructions. We put the business plan out in June of '01, and heard crickets on the thing.

People were saying, "I don't know these guys, and I don't know what they're doing. They are restaurant guys doing wine. Talk about losing money."

Jim Costello, Chris's dad, was using a lot of political capital to get this deal done. Chris was talking to all these guys—family, friends, and other people's friends, whoever he could. They revised the plan to make it more lucrative for investors. We cut down to 20 percent of the company for our shares. We also built in all these ups: promotions based on cumulative and noncumulative returns. We'd have to pay their money back, and give them 25 percent annually for a certain number of years. Then, if we hit our big target, we'd get 60 percent of the company.

I thought, "Cool. If we can get to 40, that's good."

After the first round of the offering and with the deafening sound of really large crickets, we restructured the offering to be more attractive. The second version went out on September 9, 2001. All while we had current bills to pay. Another blessing was granted to us. Some bridge financing from the core group of original investors. I don't know why they decided to risk their cash, but they did.

Kosta Browne would not have happened if not for this step.

Two days after we sent out the second version of the offering, I was driving to Lake County to check on our Sauvignon Blanc vineyard. I had my radio on, and heard the Twin Towers had come down. Of course I was shocked by the magnitude of the event and what was happening in NYC. My heart sank with the thought of the situation. Once I processed that, I thought about our deal and how it would look in the eyes of an investor in a potentially high-risk deal. And we could be on the verge of World War Three. I thought, "Well, how do we do this now?"

We had bridge loans everywhere, just trying to keep it going. No equity capital, more obligations, and I wondered how we would ever pay back these bridge loans. Somehow we squeaked out a third of the equity raise that year.

It was the same thing the next year. Some of the Class A investors wouldn't come back in, so we bumped them down to create a new Class B, which was preferred, something not typically done but we had no choice. This was the strategy of the Costellos. Very smart but certainly risky.

We got new people involved in 2002, along with the original investors, for about another third. The third year we rounded out to around 900K from the 1 million we wanted.

During our capital raise, Dan Davis, one of our investors, knew a guy named Steve Kanzler. Steve came to me and said, "I have some extra grapes and it's late in the season; would you like them?"

I told him, "I would love the grapes, but I don't have any money to buy them because we already bought another lot from a different vineyard."

Steve said, "I'll sell it to you for $2,000 a ton, and you pay me after you sell the wine. And I'll put $50,000 in your business."

Sold.

The grapes were hanging out there for a long time, longer than I'd ever seen grapes hang. It was indicative of that vineyard. I went out and tasted the grapes, and they burst with flavor. It was making sense to me. Out of nowhere, by happenstance, this taught me about picking at the right level of ripeness. One of my epiphany moments, so to speak.

Getting these grapes was such a big deal because when you start out, no one will sell you high-quality grapes because they don't know you. They don't know how you make wine or if you're reliable, and if you'll pay your bills. Steve took a shot on us, and we were really lucky for it.

And the importance became even more apparent later: that

wine ended up being the first wine that got us into the *Spectator*, with a photograph and everything.

BOUNCING BACK FROM BAD LUCK

The 2000 vintage was our second Pinot Noir; we hoped it was going to be $60,000 in revenue, mostly direct. We got the best bottles and adhered the labels ourselves. We polished them, wrapped them in tissue paper, boxed them together in custom boxes. They looked great and they were ready.

We decided to price the wine at forty-eight dollars retail, which was high at the time, but we wanted to make a statement, and the wine was very good.

Or so I thought.

I didn't know it at the time, but it was infected with Brettanomyces, and I did it unfiltered. Not what I was going for at all.

Brettanomyces is a very strong type of yeast, a spoilage yeast, which produces unpleasant aromatics and flavors (a barnyard, like I said). If it finds a trace of sugar, it will ferment in the bottle, not only producing these aromatics and flavors, but also CO_2, which makes the wine fizzy. These are major flaws in the wine, and that's what we had on our hands.

I had to sit down with Jim, Chris's dad, and say, "Hey, that big wine I was telling you about? The flagship wine that was going to launch our brand? We can't sell it."

We couldn't sell any of those bottles because it would have tarnished our brand. We couldn't come out of the gate with that wine. It wouldn't have worked. This was our reputation and if you start that way, it's a hard climb out of that hole.

Jim said, "We've just got to close this down. I'm wasting energy and political resources."

I said, "No, we're not giving up. We're going to do this. Trust in us, and we'll make this happen. This is all I've got, and we can make it happen."

I learned from that, big time. I've learned about better practices and making sure we're in a clean facility. I got rid of all the barrels, cleaned everything up. I did more lab tests, and learned what those lab tests meant. I learned how to work with wine, and how to produce clean wine.

The investors wanted to stop, but I convinced them to keep going. The better wines happened in '02. When '02 hit, we made some very good wines and got a good score on one of them.

But the biggest lot of the '02 vintage was the Sonoma

Coast...and that lot got infected, just like the 2000 did. It got infected in a different way, but the result was the same.

We bottled the wine. I did check for infection through the lab, and the wine was clean and bottle-ready, but it got reinfected somehow. We're not sure how it happened because a case would have three good ones, and then the rest would be bad. I'm thinking the bottle line wasn't properly sanitized.

We were able to sell the wine, and a lot of people liked it around the country. They especially liked it in Hong Kong, with a specific French sommelier going nuts for it. It was a great style for him and his restaurant, so we sold him a lot.

So, we got through the 2002 vintage.

TURNING THE TIDE

Despite these setbacks, we were selling wine and starting to gain some momentum. The main way we did it was by targeting underground wine blogs.

Remember, this was in the early 2000s, so online stuff was very new. I found some blogs and forums where people talked about wine, I scoped them out, identified the big players, and decided to invite them out to our place. I thought, "Let's get them out to the winery, show them a couple of experiences, show them what we're doing, and they'll market for us."

So, we did that, and it was working—we were building momentum in the underground, in the blogs, and in the forums. Our sales were about 30 percent direct to our mailing list, and the majority of these people came from those blogs. The rest of our sales would go through wholesale channels to reach wine shops and restaurants.

Doing that, we pretty much sold all of the '03 vintage, which was a good vintage—and most importantly, clean wine all the way through.

In that vintage, our wines were big and intense (at least for the conventional Pinot Noirs of that day), and I thought, "I'm gonna get killed for this because they aren't in the style that people are looking for in Pinot Noirs. They are big wines with high alcohol."

It wasn't meant to be that way. I just picked too late—I didn't get ahead of the picking schedule. Another lesson I learned: you gotta be ahead of the picking schedule, for scheduling purposes.

So, I made these big wines, and they were still fermenting six months later, but they were fine. I made those wines, and then the people came in, the wine geeks (term of endearment) we'd been fostering from the blogs and forums, the people that really tasted lots of wines and had great palates.

Honestly, at the time, I didn't know if I should have them taste the wine. I didn't want to be lambasted for making the "wrong kind" of Pinot Noir, that sort of thing. I was very sensitive to that. That's kind of the culture in Pinot Noir.

I decided I would barrel taste with them. They loved it. These people tried it and said, "Whoa, that's good! What's going on here?"

I thought we were on to something, on to a style. Everybody was saying, "Yeah, man, these are different. Really good, very flavorful. What are you doing with these?"

I told them what we were trying to do, but the God's honest truth is, at that point in my career, I didn't really know what I was doing. I wasn't trying to deceive them about what I was doing and my lack of knowledge; I just told them what I knew. I put pretty flowers around the rest, the parts I didn't know.

These were high-end tasters. I'd ask them, "What do you think?" They liked it. "Well, what do you like about it?" They'd say, "It's got depth. It's elegant, but it's intense."

That is how I came up with the term "elegant intensity."
It's our whole mantra, and I coined it fourteen years ago.
Elegant intensity. It's how I internally define our wines.

This was the evolution of the style. I want to make intense
wines, but they have to be elegant. Like my wife...she's
intense, but how does she hold herself like that? That's a
piece of artwork.

This was the tipping point, tasting the '03s with all the wine
bloggers and writers, and how we really laid the groundwork
for what happened later. We brought in people who really
cared about wine and who wrote about wine, and then we
let them try our stuff out of the barrels, and then we listened
to what they said to figure out how to describe it.

A TASTE OF SUCCESS

In 2005, I brought the '03s to the World of Pinot Noir event
in March, the same ones we barrel tasted with all the bloggers and wine writers. I tasted those wines at the event, and
suddenly, before I knew it, people were coming in and out,
and they were all digging it.

The next day, the message boards and forums exploded,
especially Robert Parker's board, The Underground. Not
Robert Parker himself, but his wine forum.

The mailing list exploded with new subscriptions, and we were the next hot thing. Wow.

You'd think this would be good. But it actually created problems for us.

Before World of Pinot Noir, we were excited about our wines, and we had a lot of people who wanted our wines, so we were able to set our allocations and basically commit all of our wine between our mailing list and the distributors.

But once everything took off at World of Pinot Noir, the demand was way ahead of supply, and this took us by surprise. We had a waiting list for our wine, for the first time ever. We were setting ourselves up for this, we wanted it, but we weren't sure how to handle it when it hit.

Dan and Chris and I got back to work. One morning in June of 2005, we were planning to go over our marketing strategies to try to figure out how we were going to evolve our business based on this new demand and how to use this opportunity the best we could.

Just before the meeting, I got a phone call from Brian Loring of Loring Wine Company, and he said, "Congratulations!"

I said, "For what?"

"You just got the best lineup of scores for Pinot Noirs ever. You got all 93 through 96s."

"What?"

I walked into the meeting, and they looked at me and said, "You look like you just saw a ghost."

I told them the news, and they looked like they saw ghosts too.

What happened from that point forward was very uncomfortable. That's the weird thing about success—it's never what you expect.

I felt like I was doing my wine thing, having people come out, doing my craftsman deal, grooving and starting to understand how to make wine. I thought that maybe in five years, I would be able to really start to know what I was doing, and that's cool. Plus the business had turned around, and we were starting to make a little money.

Then the whole place erupted based on these scores. We got the best lineup of scores ever for an American Pinot Noir, and all of a sudden everyone in the wine business had an opinion about us. Blogs were going up everywhere, we had lovers and haters, and it was just insane.

It was all of a sudden. I felt like I was in the middle of a stadium, and the stadium lights had been turned on, and they were all pointed directly at us. But when the lights are on you, you can't see anyone in the audience, you know? It was the weirdest feeling, very uncomfortable. I didn't like it.

Honestly—it was too much, too soon. I didn't know what I was doing yet. I had a lot to learn. And I still do. It's a never-ending thing, but then, I was really inexperienced.

My first thought was, "Oh man, I have to do this again. I can't mess this up. We can't be a flash in the pan."

You get one good vintage, and you're hot. Then, if you have a bad vintage, everyone asks, "What happened to the wines? Who messed up?"

Not to mention how it impacted sales. Everything was sold out immediately. Done and gone.

But it got worse when it came time to ship the wines.

Chris sent the spreadsheet to our shipping company after we sold the 2003 wines, and somehow the Excel file transferred incorrectly. It doubled everyone's allocation.

So, if you were supposed to get six bottles, you got twelve.

Without finding the mistake, they started fulfilling orders and shipping them out.

Then we realized, "We're out of wine, and we're only half-way done?"

We checked the warehouse. It was all gone. Then, we started getting phone calls from people saying they received too much wine. Since we had already sold it, we had to ask for them to ship it back.

It was a nightmare situation.

We had to pay for shipping and all the wine coming back. Plus we were on the phone with everyone, trying to get this smoothed over. We had a lot of very upset consumers. A lot of them were willing to even pay for the extra wine, but we couldn't do that. We had NO extra wine that year. We thanked everyone for their patience and told them we were going to move them to the top of the list next year.

This was a major deal. Chalk another one up to learning.

Then the '04 vintage happened. I'd learned a lot about vineyards and winemaking, and I was ready for the vintage. Mind you, I was still making wine at THREE locations: Deerfield's small winery in Kenwood, a custom crush facility in Santa Rosa, and Kosta Browne in Sebastopol.

I can't believe I didn't get any speeding tickets.

The '04 vintage was similar to the '03 in that it was hot during harvest. I missed some of the picking windows, so the fruit hung longer than I would have liked and got very ripe. The resulting wines were big and intense, something I was hoping to scale back from the '03 vintage a bit to refine the wines.

And then there was the pressure. I thought, "Damn, man, I need to get some good scores here. 90s won't be good enough." I had to at least get like 93s, minimum.

Then, during blending, I caught a cold. I couldn't smell or taste anything. I put it in my mouth, and just felt the texture. So, I went purely on texture alone for the '04 blending. This was another lesson learned about texture, and now, to this day, that is what I look for the most: mouthfeel.

We bottled them up, and I sent them in for review to the *Wine Spectator*.

So, I submitted the wines. I was scared to death. I was afraid we would be a flash in the pan, and I am always my own worst critic. But we had to do it.

We found out a month later we got better scores than the '03—95, 96, 97, 98.

There had only been one other Pinot Noir to ever score a 98 in the history of the *Wine Spectator*. Now there were two.

We got these high scores, which was epic for our brand, and all I could think was, "Oh my God, I have to do this again next year."

Here we go again, tiger by the tail. You get a success and think it's cool, but then there's work to do, a lot of work. There's no time to sit there. You're only as good as your latest wine.

MORE SUCCESS, MORE WORK

By the time we got to the '05 vintage, the rocket had taken off. Except I was not fully on it.

I was still making wine in three different locations and had five guys working with me, who were all new to wine. I was still making wines for Deerfield Ranch through '05 because I needed to make a living. It was insane the amount of work I was doing just to get by. People think one success means you are set. Not in the wine business.

Kosta Browne was paying me, but not enough. It was like $50,000. After we got the highest American Pinot scores in 2004, I quit all of that. I started making a bit more money so I could shed my restaurant job and my winemaking job at Deerfield. I needed to focus on the business and also provide for my family. Skinny times, but we did it. Wine is a capital-intensive business; it took me that long to even get one paying position that could support our family, even with all that success.

Then, the market started taking off. Dan was out there selling and marketing wine, and Chris was making sure the finances were set with investors and working on bank deals. That's when we got our first bank loan. Silicon Valley Bank came in. We had a good relationship with them, and we needed more capital that year—we were 30 percent over grapes.

2005 was a big year in terms of quantity and production, large clusters, and I underestimated the yields. We made about 30 percent more wine that year than we had planned. So we needed more money to make that wine.

We needed just $200,000 more to pay the grapes bill. Then there were bottling costs. And barrels and all of that. We made it all because there was demand for it. I think it was a total of 7,000 cases at that time. We got through that, and the wines were cool. I still love the '05; it was just a fantastic vintage for Pinot Noir, thank God.

The next year was hard. The thing I remember most about '06 is confrontation. We were still making wine at the Deerfield location. Some of the crew at Deerfield did not get along with some of my crew. Which is normal. There's lots of intensity at harvest, and this was the most wine that had ever been made at that facility at that time.

Frustrations were running high. One of the guys on my team was a hothead, and he would get pissed off. One day he threw a chair across the crush pad. I said, "Hey, man, there's no throwing chairs." It was like *Jerry Springer* in there.

Another one of the guys on my team put dry ice and water in plastic bottles. You throw that, and it goes off like an M-80. I had another intern drinking too much. He lived in a tent at Deerfield because he couldn't afford anything else. He would kind of trip out, get his bow and arrow, and start shooting at trees. Once, we were sitting on a crush pad and a little wine tank was next to us. We were all talking and suddenly we hear a "Bing!" We were on the ground, and it hit the tank right next to our heads. We were sitting right there. The guy said, "Don't worry, I got it." I'm thinking, "Really, dude?" But we had to keep making wine.

So '06 turned out to have a bigger crop yield than '05, but it was not the best vintage. We had all this fruit that kept coming. We made some cool wines, but it was probably my personal least favorite vintage throughout our history.

We got through that vintage, and we decided we needed our

own place. We got a warehouse, a former processing plant, built our own little 18,000-square-foot winery. It was one room, and we renovated and split it into three rooms. It worked well for what we needed at the time, and we finally had our own facility, which was a very big deal to us.

We made the '07 vintage there, the first one we made at our own winery. The '07s were beautiful wines; it was a fantastic vintage. I finally started getting up on my craft, and my associate winemaker was bringing in some great ideas. Our team was finally working as a unit to get this thing up and going, professionally, rather than just duct tape and chewing gum. We made some fantastic wines that year.

My goal with each vintage is to be the best Pinot Noir in that vintage. Every producer deals with the same weather each year; I just want to make the best wines with that weather and let that vintage shine through.

Then, '08 happened. It was similar to the '05 vintage in terms of the cluster size. The wines were very good, not the best, but very good. I was more than happy with the resulting wines from '08; in fact, it was the best Amber Ridge Pinot Noir I ever made.

Through that, we got a bit of an increase in production. Business was still going, still growing, and we were getting a lot of sign-ups.

Then the '09 vintage happened, and we were really starting to dial in every aspect of our game. Our marketing efforts were doing great, our production facility was working well, our winemaking was leveling up; all of it was working.

In 2009 we got really good grapes. It was a great vintage. Mother Nature was shining down on us.

We made a slew of '09s that were excellent. I finished all of the blends, except for the final one, which was the Sonoma Coast, the biggest lot that year and the biggest lot we had ever made at that point.

For Wine of the Year, *Wine Spectator* looks at a few things: production level, score, price point, and the X factor (as they call it), which is buzz about the brand, excitement for the wine, that sort of thing.

As I was blending the Sonoma Coast, I thought to myself, "This is a dynamite wine. Score should be on our side. Price is right as well, fifty-two dollars a bottle. Production level is great at two thousand cases. The X factor is right there, as we've been in the top twenty three times already. With all of that, we are in good position to get the number one wine this vintage."

They do a countdown, by day. Number ten, not us. Number seven. Number four, not us. Then, it got down to number two. Oh, we didn't get it.

We didn't get number two, so did we totally miss it, or did we get it? Either we didn't make the top ten, or we're number one. I was betting on number one.

The next day, boom—we got it. Way bigger than top ten. International people were calling us; the world was trying to get this wine. That put Kosta Browne on the world stage.

The '09 Sonoma Coast. Number one wine in the world.

All I could think about was, "Man, I hope the '10s are good."

CHAPTER 7

THE BUSINESS MODEL

MOST SUCCESSFUL PEOPLE, ONCE THEY GET SUCCESS-ful, make up a bunch of stories to explain why they succeeded. Those stories are usually wrong. They don't actually explain what really happened; they are just a bunch of clichés to make them look good.

I don't want to do that. I think we built on our success in an unconventional way of doing business, but I want to lay it out in a way that is honest about how we got here.

To try and convey that, I am laying this section out in an unusual way. I will walk you through the major points that I think contributed to the development of our way of doing things.

The "Kosta Browne" business model has been pretty effective for us. But we did not come up with this ahead of time. So much of our success was a combination of trial and error, lucky timing, and a strict adherence to our personal values.

To understand our model, you kind of have to walk through these turning points and feel them the way we did.

PINOT NOIR: THE EPIPHANY

Wines that blow your head off are called "epiphany wines."

When I was in my early twenties, I was into Zinfandels and Cabernets—big reds and big wines. Most of the Pinot Noirs I tried sucked.

One of my wine mentors, Larry Van Aalst, taught me a lot about wine. He said, "Michael, red wine's all about Pinot Noir." Like a stupid kid, I replied, "No, it's not. Pinot Noirs suck."

I was twenty-one at that time. I knew nothing.

He said, "Trust me, if you find the right one, it will blow your mind."

I said, "Whatever, man. I know what I want. I want big, jammy reds."

Williams Selyem was very popular then. All direct sales from the winery to customers and restaurants, no discount. It was allocated and highly sought-after. It was the first one of its kind in California. The model was brilliant. You couldn't get it; you couldn't find the guys to buy it from.

One time I was hanging out with friends, and Burt Williams's daughter, Margie Williams, showed up with a half case of open bottles from a tasting she did earlier at their winery. She brought them out, and boom, boom, boom. We went through a few of these wines, and they were good. They had some substance to them. It wasn't thin, wimpy, anorexic Pinot like I'd always had before. They were delicious with great character.

Then she pulled out a bottle of '91 Allen Vineyard Pinot Noir. It was 1996 at the time.

I poured a glass, smelled it, and I was like, "Whoa, hold on."

I put it in my mouth and felt it on my palate, and it was like my head spun off my shoulders, then reattached in a slightly different way but very firmly in place. It gave me a different perspective.

The flavor was like a big bowl of cherries, strawberries, and spice. It had this Pinot Noir elixir focus I'd never experienced. I can still see it clearly in my mind, and taste it on my palate. The textures really blew me away, something I've never experienced before in any wine. It was the supreme expression of Pinot Noir, with the finest of details.

From that moment on, I was all about Pinot. I knew I would make a wine like that someday, and chase after those types of wines. They are rare—you can't find them.

If I had a wine and winemaker that I modeled myself after the most, it was the older Williams Selyem, and the style of winemaker Burt Williams.

The older ones were a similar style to us and struck a chord with people. Like I said, it was originally Burt Williams that got me into Pinot. Those wines were special, and I think the Kosta Browne style was most influenced by them.

Since then, I've gotten to know Burt Williams. When there was a celebration of his life, I was one of the speakers who honored him, and I told the story about the epiphany wine, the '91 Allen Vineyard.

He came up to me afterward and told me he still had three bottles left. We planned to drink a bottle together, but have yet to do so. I look forward to that day.

Bob Cabral, a friend of mine who ran Williams Selyem for sixteen years, gave me a bottle. I'm never going to open it.

That wine changed my life.

ALL ABOUT PINOT

One of the big questions I get from people is something along the lines of, "How did you guys know Pinot Noir was the future? How did you get on that train so much earlier than other people?"

In '97, when we first started making wine, Pinots weren't that big of a deal. People were into Cabs, and Americans didn't understand Pinot Noir.

But at John Ash & Co., some of our most savvy wine con sumers came in looking for California Pinot Noir. There weren't that many of them, you know? We loved Pinot Noir, and we were down with it, and I took notice of this—people who really knew wine and had a very evolved, sophisticated palate in wine wanted more California Pinot Noir. This was a rare group, and I paid attention to them.

Also, it was growing in our backyard, in the Russian River Valley. Some of the best stuff from California, and the world, came right out of there. There was a niche market, a need for it. People wanted more.

My thought process was that if we could get a brand that did 2,000-3,000 cases a year, we could make a living off that.

We had a vision to rent and outfit a barn, put in a sound system, play Rush's *2112*, make wine, sell it, and that would be cool. We were down with that. That's what we seriously wanted to do.

If we grew beyond that, that was cool with us, but we didn't want to get ahead of ourselves, right?

We wanted to do Pinot Noir, but we realized pretty quickly that it would be very expensive to do it right. It would be tied up for a long time. That's why we did Sauvignon Blanc first, because Sauvignon Blancs were taking off, and they didn't need to be aged. It was far less capital intensive. We could turn the revenue before the next year's harvest.

But ultimately, we loved Pinot Noir, and it was here. It grew well here. There was an unmet market for it, and there was more demand than there was supply. That was why we decided early on that we wanted to be a Pinot Noir producer.

Then the movie *Sideways* came out in '04, and we got all these big scores in '05. You couldn't have scripted it better. You couldn't. We made that decision eight years prior to go all in on Pinot Noir, but it was pure luck on our part that the movie coincided with our wine taking off.

The inherent problem with good quality Pinot Noir is it's very expensive to grow. There's a lot of work involved. It's a crop level thing. You can grow Cab at five tons an acre and make pretty good stuff. Pinot takes much less than that, and very fine-tuned farming. We often pull two tons or less an acre. That is very expensive.

Then you get into the thin-skinned aspect of it. You have to lay it in soft—it's fairly delicate for wine grapes. Some people say Pinot Noir is the hardest to make. It is if you treat it like it's just any red varietal. It takes finesse and demands respect. You can't overwork the wine; you have to learn to be at one with the wine, and let it be what it is.

That's another thing that appealed to me about Pinot Noir, as a craftsman—that it is unique. You have to be fine-tuned in all aspects, and you have to be willing to risk and become vulnerable in the pursuit of letting it be what it is.

Everyone always says it's a heartbreak grape: it's really hard to nail it, and it's hard to get it done. I like that high-precision angle.

So many wine people think they have to start with other grapes first. Why would I start somewhere else and then work my way up? Why not start there, rip the Band-Aid off and go for it, you know? If that's what I want to do, then why don't I just do it? No training wheels.

The way I think about it is, if you're going to do something, do it the best you can. If it's difficult, learn from the difficulties and try to figure out how to perfect it. Or at least try. Perfection doesn't exist, but you can try to get close to it.

Why mess around with other grapes that might be easier to grow, or other wines that might be easier to make? If it's the hardest thing, I want to go for that. It's nice for some things to be easy, but as a profession or craft, or something I do with my hands and mind, I want to stretch a bit.

It's like getting on that trapeze. Stretch a bit. Figure it out. Ride the bike on the tightrope.

WE DID IT OUR WAY (WITH SOME HELP)

I wasn't a professional winemaker first. I didn't receive training to make wine, or get a sommelier certification. I got into winemaking because I love the grape and what the grape made.

Yes, that was a pain in the ass at times. I literally didn't even know how to clean a barrel. But like I said, I turned this disadvantage into an advantage and used my inexperience to figure out the very best way to do things, not the way everyone else did them.

That's just the way I think. I'm not sure why, but I don't like to run with the main crowd. I don't like to follow what others are doing.

For example, even though I like to learn from people with experience, I won't do things exactly the same way they did them. I used to take bits and pieces of what other winemakers did, and implement it. Whenever I had a problem, I called a few winemakers I respected and said, "Hey, I've got this problem, what do you think?"

They'd give me different answers, and I would pick out the parts that made sense to me. Then implement it.

Did it work? Great.

Did it fail? OK, I'll fine-tune it somehow and keep practicing it until it works.

Doing it that way helped me get a handle on winemaking in a way that someone who just learns from a textbook or imitates others never will.

When you go through life like this, people look at you like you're kind of nutty because it doesn't fit into their mold.

But here's the thing about wine (and life, really): there's no mold.

The idea that there is a mold you have to fit into, a "right way" to do things, is just an illusion. Yeah, some ways are better than others, but there's no such thing as "the" right way.

I like the no mold thing, because what's life without that? How boring would it be if we were all the same?

If you open yourself up to the seemingly impossible, or the things that are difficult, it will be hard in the short term, but man, at least in my life, it was far more rewarding overall. I know during the pain you think, "Oh, no, that's too painful," or, "I don't want to go through that." I thought the same thing at times.

But I would discover after I went through it that it was actually kind of cool.

I can't tell you how many times I thought, "Wow, I never would have known if I didn't try it."

CONNECTING WITH PEOPLE TO MARKET THE WINE

Dan and I got lucky in that we started right about the time the internet came into existence. So we started with the place we saw the most excited, eager, and authentic people: wine blogs and forums. Those people seemed like our people. They loved wine, they loved to geek out about it and study it, and they seemed to really be into wine for the sake of wine.

So we invited those people to our place, we had tastings with them, and we got to know them. We wanted to show people who cared about wine what we were trying, and be real about it. We tried to tap into their soul in a way that was comfortable for them, and share part of our soul with them. People like to sit around the fire, break bread, and drink wine. That's part of being human.

I believe there's an opportunity there for anyone to do this, but it's gotta be authentic and real. Make somebody slow down. Give them the opportunity to do so through a bottle of wine, music, dinner, and friends, whatever. We're just an element, a part of that, but people have been using wine to connect for at least 5,000 years.

There might be somebody who sits there and geeks out on a bottle of wine all night, but mostly it's just part of the other things. If you can tell stories, give them an experience that brings them closer to that part of their DNA, one that feels good and cozy, then your wine is associated with a great experience.

When they open that wine, they're going to say, "Oh, yeah, I like this. Remember the time, Judy, when we had the Kosta Browne bottle with our friends in Colorado?" We get that all the time. People say, "Hey, we had your wine here, here's a picture of me and my wife with the bottle."

It's not just a bottle of wine—there's more to it. If you can portray that in a way that's authentic, that they understand, and makes them feel good, they will want to buy it.

I mean, we're in business to sell product, but if you can go beyond that to a point where it's more about the bottle of wine as an experience, an emotion, it makes sense. The wine becomes a tool to facilitate a great experience and a meaningful connection. That's a deep desire we all have, and if we can help make that happen with our wine, that's the best marketing there is.

We wanted our wine to facilitate people's memories and experiences. It wasn't a strategy of ours early on. It was just our values as people. We wanted to be authentic. We wanted to be real, because that's who we are.

We didn't want to have a big, egotistical, arrogant impression with our brand. That's not us.

Things kind of evolved from there. We just wanted to make a really good wine, tell people about it, get into it with them, and show people different aspects of the wine, because it's fun to talk about. Over time, it became more of my personal spin and understanding of what we wanted to portray as a brand.

That's the whole goal of our marketing today with Cirq: deeply connect with the process of making wine so we can do cool things, then share those things with people who care in an authentic way, and use that wine to help them have meaningful experiences. That's it.

FIGHTING THE FLOW OF RETAIL

The question of how and where to sell your wine is integral to any business model.

If you sell a bottle of wine traditionally in retail outlets, you can get wide distribution. That's good. The problem is that it's 50 percent off retail, you only make half the money.

We set on a strategy to sell our wines direct to consumers and make 95 percent of the money. That's a big percentage difference. You can almost double your profitability.

So why doesn't everyone sell direct to consumers?

Because it is MUCH harder to do.

The downside of that is, building a brand that is strong enough to do that, and then creating and maintaining those customer relationships, takes a lot of time and effort. It's so much easier to just connect with a distributor and let them handle everything and sell your wine. You just make less money. Although there is nothing easy about that either.

It's easier for consumers too. Most people just want to go to the store or wine shop and just get their wine. It's immediate gratification. Direct to consumer means something like, "Oh, I got an email, then I have to wait two or three years, then I get another email. Then I have to go online and get it, and I have to make sure I'm there for shipping. And then what if it's warm?" It's a pain in the ass.

But, consumers are into it, *if you do it right*.

If they know that's the only way to get it, and the wine is worth it, they will go through all of that. In fact, it adds to the experience if you do it right. It makes the wine more special.

If we had all these wine shops selling Cirq, people would say, "Screw it, Joe's down the street has it. Why am I going to go through you?"

It's imperative to be in certain restaurants, mainly for marketing. You always need to be present. I've always wanted to be the most expensive American Pinot Noir on the list. In some places, we are.

That's how we are now. The vast majority of our sales is through our list, with a very limited amount through restaurants and an even smaller amount through wine shops.

Now, when we started Kosta Browne, we were definitely selling wine to distributors. We had to for a while, of course, because no one knew us. It took us time, and a lot of awards for good wine, to get to the point where we could sell almost totally to our list.

But even then, when we were selling to distributors, we had to fight this insidious creep of dilution of our brand. We had a single brand focus: Pinot Noir. I studied the high-end brands, and they were the same way. It's not a shotgun approach—it's a sniper shot. Pick your target and hit it. You don't want to go shotgun and blast every varietal possible out there and just hope you hit something.

All these distributors said, "Well, you can't just sell Pinot Noir. You got a Chardonnay, or something else? A Zinfandel? You have to have a portfolio." We said, "We're making Pinot Noir. It's what we do."

A lot of people said it wouldn't work. You know what that did? It just added fuel to the fire. I thought, "OK, we'll see if it doesn't work."

MARKETING AND POSITIONING

Marketing and positioning is very complex. We do it in a lot of different ways.

Obviously, it starts with quality. I'm not talking about score quality, though that definitely helps. I'm talking about the pleasure of the consumer and how they enjoy the wine. If you don't have that, forget about anything else.

Is it delicious? Is it going to taste good? It's got to be accessible, with no other information. All the information is from your nose, your palate, and your senses.

You have to do it in your style. You can't try to mimic someone else's style, or say, "Oh, these people like this, I'll make wine for them."

Some people make wines just for the reviewers alone. They do it well, and it's cool, but you have to be true to what it is. Hopefully there are enough people that like that style.

My thing is the deliciousness. It has to be delicious. You have to taste the wine and say, "Wow, that was really delicious. I enjoyed that." In my opinion, it has to start there.

I said for many years that I want to appeal to novice wine drinkers. I want them to think, "Man, that was good. I've never had a wine that good."

Then, I also want to appeal to the top-notch palates of the world, and get them saying, "Wow, for that style, they are nailing that."

It doesn't matter if they like that style or not; they will just say we are nailing that style. Some of these people love it, some of them don't, but hopefully they will respect it for what it is.

In my opinion, you've got to hit both ends. Quality, in that way, is how I look at it. It's a balance. This is all about balance in many ways.

Don't get me wrong; this is not the only way to have a successful wine business. It's just the way we do it, to be successful in our style and in our methods of marketing. There are all kinds of successful wines that do something different.

There are so many ways to do branding and positioning, so I don't want to make it seem like our way is the only way, or even the best way.

Here's the thing: almost any brand can work, if you are using the right brand for the right space. You need to have authenticity, especially in the luxury space. That's what we're in, the luxury space.

That's where I like to play. There's a bit of mystery involved. You have to think, you have to hunt a little bit. People don't want to hunt for nothing. They want to be enticed to hunt for something. Then, it's got to be an authentic brand with meaning.

You have the quality, authentic brand with meaning, and then you aim for the right audience. If you have a really good quality wine, a good brand, you think, "Let's get it into all these restaurants and wine shops." Well, it's just like every other wine, then. The brand equity takes a long time to build up. In luxury, it's all about quality and scarcity.

We wanted to hit the market that's very discerning. Once you tap into these little groups, these cells around the country and world, you will know. It's portrayed by them asking, "Oh, wow, really? What is that again? Huh? I want that. I've got the best watch in the world, but I want that wine."

For example, take the story of one of our early customers. He was at a restaurant where one of my friends was the sommelier. My friend recommended Kosta Browne, which he had never heard of. It was from '02 vintage. He says, "This is what I've been looking for. It reminds me of the older burgundies I used to love. Now, they're all different. I want more."

So he calls his assistant. "Get me this Kosta Browne." This guy can buy anything he wants. She says, "I've got good news, and bad news. The bad news is, there's none out there to buy. The good news is, you're number 12,462 on the list." He says, "What?"

All of a sudden, he's like, "I want that wine." This guy, the guy who can buy anything in the world, can't get our wine. That made him even more into it—but first, he had to really like the wine itself.

Scarcity aside, there's an audience for it, but it's hard

to tap into that audience. That's where the networking comes in. Then you start meeting all these people that are tapping into different networks, and it's really cool how it works.

They introduce it to their friends. They want to be the person that introduces something cool to their friends. Networking: that's the angle on the whole direct-to-consumer model. It doesn't matter what it costs. A lot of times, when it's more expensive, they want it even more. But it's hard to get in there in the sea of wines, although the channel is wide open if you do it right.

It's wide open if you're good enough and do everything right. You have to have a pedigree, a certain amount. You have to have a benchmark. People have to see that you are good craftsmen, and that you handmade this for them. They have to see that you are real.

CUSTOMER SERVICE

Customer service is important in every business, but in the high-end wine business, it is crucial. We hammer this all the time to our staff, but you have to really be vigilant on this or things get messed up, and it deeply impacts what your customers think.

I'll give you an example: we made a mistake during one of

our offerings on the "save the date" email. We had about 2,000 new slots open on our list. We sent communication to 2,000 people who had just signed up on the list (which usually means they have about three years to wait for wines), instead of the 2,000 people who were next and had been waiting for years.

We didn't have the wine to sell to those people that year. It had already been allocated. We could NOT sell the wine to those 2,000 who had just signed up.

Someone suggested sending them an email telling them this. No. Rather than sending an email, we wanted to do a hand-signed letter. There were a lot of them. It is hard to sign 2,000 letters. But we did it.

So, overnight, we drafted a letter and apologized for the mistake, said it was a glitch in our system. We promised to move them up early the next year. We couldn't that year because we just didn't have the wine. Chris, Dan, and I sat down and signed every letter by hand. It took forever.

As soon as we sent those out, about one hundred people dropped. OK, that happens. We tried.

On the flip side of that, one person who ran a college business program wanted to put the letter in her next textbook. She wanted to use it as an example of excellent customer service. She said you usually don't see things like this. Mark that one in the success column.

That's just one example, but the point is that customer service in our model is all about the details. The details are what differentiate us.

You've got to do the little things like letters to bring them to the fire (I call it the fire, you know, sitting around the fire). We have to bring people here, give them attention, and give them details. Yes, we have thousands and thousands of customers; it's our mainstay. But we have thousands of customers because we treat them nicely, and when they need something, we get on it right away.

We're in the business of making good wine and delivering it well. It's hard to translate that to someone who doesn't get it. It can be fatiguing focusing on the details, but that's what needs to be done. When they say it's good enough, no, stop, let's do it right. If you don't do it right, we lose that edge, that element of connection. In the long term, it's worth it to do those extra steps.

For example, this instrument company called Sweetwater provided excellent customer service. I bought something for my son that cost $250; it wasn't a big purchase.

Two days later, someone from the company called me. "Hi,

it's Joe from Sweetwater. I just wanted to check in and let you know your order is being shipped." A week later, he called again. "How's the product? Is it working well? Do you like it?"

He called again about a month later. He was just checking in. He wasn't being pushy with sales or anything like that; he was just providing good customer service. That is perfect.

There's another thing about this. We don't want to be arrogant about it, but we also don't want to hassle people. If you don't order, that's OK, we won't pester you about it. But we have to allocate that wine to someone else on the list. If you want back on, let us know. We'll look up your history, and you're back on as soon as we have the wine. We want them to be customers, but we can't predict why they didn't buy the wine.

I'll give you an example of how we messed this up: one time, we ran a re-engagement campaign for former buyers who dropped off the list. It was a disaster.

I read blogs, and of course I saw a ton of comments like, "Yeah, I've been off the list for ten years, and they just sent me an email asking me if I want to get back on. I knew it was coming. Now Kosta Browne needs to sell wine, I guess they are no longer allocated."

We should never have re-engaged those customers in that

way and to the extent that we did; we just wanted to make sure we weren't missing someone who wanted the wine, because we value our previous customers.

At the very most, we'll do something like, if they are normally a very consistent buyer but they miss an offering, we ask about it. Maybe they're out of the country. Who knows? We send them a message: "Mr. Jones, we saw you didn't reply. You've been a buyer for five years. We just want to make sure you are receiving our communications, and if you don't want the wine, that's OK. We don't want to bug you."

Phrase it nicely. We don't want to bother them with all of these emails. If we don't hear from them, we might send one more message. After that, we put them in the sleeper zone. They're inactive. We still have their information, so if they call, we can take notes on what we did and then re-add them if they want.

Some will say, "Damn, I totally spaced it. I'm busy." We know people have busy lives. They get our email amidst a thousand. But some people don't want us to bother them. If we do bother them, they think, "What the heck? You're selling." We don't sell wine; we make wine.

We try to teach our staff to put themselves in the shoes of the person getting the wine. Maybe the person just got divorced, or is changing jobs. How are they going to react?

This is one of their coveted things, but they are too busy to deal with it.

All of a sudden, they have us harassing them? They want us to leave them alone; they have too much other stuff going on.

The data we have on them is just a computer screen—it's not the person, so I teach our staff to think about what it's like to be the person on the other side.

Interpreting the feeling and emotion of the consumer, the way they would see it, is very important. All these little aspects have to do with that. We have thousands of customers, so it's very challenging.

But that is the attention to detail that makes our model work.

IT'S NOT JUST ABOUT THE WINE

It's not just about wine quality, but it's about delivery of service and product. When they got it home, was it OK? What was it like to deal with the actual product when you got it? Was the packaging intact and respectful to the product? Was the wine cool to the touch?

We try to keep all of that in mind and make things as easy as possible for the consumer.

What does the customer see? What will they remember about this experience? How will they feel about it? Do they feel like they were taken care of? This isn't just a wine business—it's a service business too.

It all revolves around that. You can make the best product in the world, but if you don't market and deliver it correctly, people get turned off.

You can have the highest quality wine, but it's not going to be enough. You can be a hermit on the hill making the best wine in the world, but if nobody hears about it, then nobody knows about it.

This is a situation like with my friend, who owns a well-known winery.

For many years he's been making spectacular wines and sold out every year. It was a great business.

The problem is that he's an introvert—he didn't like people coming around. He said, "My business is fine; I'm selling everything. I don't like people coming around. I'm just going to make the wine, you buy it, I'll ship it to you. That's it."

Well, he disassociated the emotion and the connection from his consumer, so the consumer started to fade away. Just making great wine isn't enough. You have to connect the wine to an emotion.

He came to me one day and said, "Michael, I want to come taste your wine and talk to you about the wine business," and I go, "What?"

He's been doing this a lot longer than I have, and I have huge respect for him, and now he's asking me for advice? Talk about a humbling experience.

He comes in, and he starts talking about marketing. I say, "Oh yeah, there's a problem there. You shut your doors and stopped talking to people, so nobody comes back, right? You're not Willy Wonka. You've got to engage people."

You can see his winery from the road. It's beautiful. But, he wouldn't let anyone engage, so he got no press, he kind of faded away, and people forgot about him, even though he was making really good wines.

I asked him why he didn't submit his wines, and he goes, "Yeah, I just don't send them in anymore; he gave me some bad reviews one time."

I'm like, "Well, was the wine good or bad?"" He laughed. "Yeah, it was a bad year."

I told him he should get back into dealing with people. It would help. And maybe send his wines in for review.

He eventually did send his wines in, and a couple years after that, he got some exceptional scores, and has been getting great scores ever since.

You don't have to do everything we do to be good in wine. But you have to get out there to some extent.

If you make a killer wine, but you shut off that emotional connection—any connection at all with your consumer—they'll go fill that need somewhere else.

Connection is a part of the wine, especially when it's above a certain price point. For high-priced wine, you expect a certain level of quality and a little something special, like a story or something relatable.

You expect a connection to something more.

The flip side of this is the wine brands that spend little time on wine quality and market the hell out of it. That doesn't work either, especially not at the high end where customers are increasingly sophisticated.

You have to make great wine and connect it to something that matters. Only then can you succeed.

CHAPTER 8

STORYTELLING, TASTINGS, AND CONNECTING WITH PEOPLE

THIS SECTION COULD HAVE BEEN PART OF THE LAST chapter, but I wanted to split it out.

I feel like how we connect with people, how we tell our story and how we interact with people, how we create and maintain authentic relationships, is such an important part of our success and what we do that it needed its own section to really dive in to get the full details.

TELLING OUR STORY

Like I told you, we started everything in '97. But the most

important thing was what we did with it at John Ash, under the table. We poured it for cool people, learned what people really liked, and learned how to tell our story.

At the time, I was a sommelier and bartender. Dan was managing the place, and he did the wine program. We kept our wine in the cellar, and we would offer it to cool people that came in—it wasn't on the menu.

Here's the scene: a restaurant is controlled chaos. I didn't set out a strategy every night, thinking, "I'm going to pour this wine." Opportunity would present itself.

If a customer had a good vibe and good energy, or if they seemed laid-back and kind of into it, we would offer them our wine. If they seemed like they would be OK with breaking some rules, and I had a certain feeling about them, I'd make the offer. If they were having a good time and I could tell, for whatever reason, that they would dig something like that, they were game. I'd wait for an opportunity with those people to introduce the "bootleggy stuff." These types of people really liked that, and were then willing to try something they hadn't seen, and it added to the overall experience of the evening.

We never pushed it, but if they seemed like they wanted to try new things, we'd offer it. But we were very careful who we offered it to. It wasn't about staying out of trouble. For us, it was about market testing the wine with the people we wanted as customers.

Some people would say, "I want a Merlot." If they weren't picky and just wanted me to choose any wine, they weren't a good fit. I picked a solid wine for those people and was cool to them, but no special wine.

If they were doing a business lunch and just trying to show off what they could buy, or bragged they had met a certain famous Napa producer, they weren't the type of person I would approach.

But if someone was very inquisitive about wine and they were really into it or excited about it, they were a good candidate. If they asked for a specific brand, and wanted to discuss that, or if they wanted to get into burgundy, then that was a different story. These were the people who really knew wine. We wanted to talk to them, show them what we had done.

The other group I offered our wine to was the ultra wine geeks (like me). The type of people that would say, "I want some Montrachet." They know what they want. The people who wanted to explore. They were excited, and I could see this energy in them.

I'd ask them if they wanted to try something we made. We

didn't put our label on those bottles, so they were shiners. We'd pull a shiner out, and they'd think it was cool.

If a table seemed like they'd dig the story and the wine, I'd tickle them a bit and ask, "Want to try something special?" Then I'd walk away and leave them alone.

Ten minutes later they'd ask me, "Where's that something special?" I'd say, "Oh, yeah, I mentioned that, didn't I? Hold on, I have to go over here." Then, they'd ask again. "OK, coming right up." I wouldn't charge them for it.

We saw a hole in the Pinot market, but we didn't seek people out. It was more of an attitude. A lot of people seeking out Pinots at that time had an exploratory attitude. I never brought it up to other wine people or sommeliers, because they were beyond the novelty of homemade wine. They'd been there, done that. So, I only approached someone if they were cool, and they wanted to try something new. We just asked the customers that seemed excited about it.

One of the things we did that I think was so important was not focusing on the trophy hunters, or people just out to impress others. We only poured it for real customers. It was fun to share it with them, and it was a way to gauge what they were feeling—what they thought about the wine. It was both a market test, and a marketing test.

We'd say, "Check this out. What do you think of the style? What do you think of the flavor, and the nose?" Then, you'd take it all in. I viewed it as market research. Every time I think of that niche market, whenever I talk about it, a picture of that dining room full of people enters my mind. I think of the situation, too, because that's where it all spawned.

Then, you tell a little story about it because everyone's busy and you only have little snippets of time here and there. So, I would tell the story in little bursts over the span of an hour. When you deliver it like that, it builds anticipation to the big reveal. You build and escalate it. And then after you escalate, you have to deliver. It has to be good at the end, or the anticipation was for nothing.

I do the same thing at the winery because we have two or three hours with the guests. We have to build that anticipation with our guests, then we have to deliver a great wine when they actually taste it, one that hits all of their senses.

I noticed something: people thought the wine was really tasty, but they were *more* into the story than the wine.

The story I told was "Hey, we started making our own wine in a garage. We saved our tips for months and bought some grapes on East Side Road. We bought a hand-cranked destemmer, worked with that, and got it done. We knew just enough to create what you're tasting. We only have twenty-four cases of this. Tell me what you think."

Then we're right there serving the wine to them. Suddenly, what we're pouring is more interesting because it has a story.

We still tell that story. I keep telling it. Not only because it's true, but because it resonates with people. I'll probably tell it forever, when appropriate, of course. Everyone in the wine business has probably heard it, but that's a small population. The people in the wine business are not our customers. We have to keep telling the story to expand the circle. Most people aren't wine people and haven't even heard about our brand at all, let alone the story behind it.

I also continue to tell the same story because it's the truth—it's what we did. I didn't grow up in the wine business. People asked how long we have been in the business, and I would tell them, "Two years." They assumed I came from a wine family. It surprises people who have a perceived set of assumptions of who makes wine.

No, we were unknowns. It's a true story from some randoms, and it has worked in such a big way.

The majority of the reactions I got to the story were something I didn't expect. Everyone wanted to tell me about their dream: "That's cool, man. I've been wanting to do my thing forever." I would ask them, "Why not do it?"

I feel like part of the reason the story works so well is that in everyone's heart of hearts, they want to do something like this. It might not be wine; it might be music or golf or whatever, but they want to go follow their dream and create something they love.

Some will go out there and do it. Some wish they would've done it, and for others it may not have even crossed their minds. But it resonates with people for that reason.

We had no idea that would happen.

People ask me all the time if I thought it would be like this. Hell no. It's way bigger than I ever thought it would be. My dream was to have a bungalow in the hills where I could hang out with cool people. I couldn't afford a lot of wines, but if I could make one, I would have all the wine I needed.

CONVENTIONAL TOURS AND TASTINGS

I have always refused to do a public, open tasting room. By-appointment tastings always resonated more with me.

I don't want to have a public tasting room for a high-end luxury brand. To me, that kills it. Then it's all about sales, and you start pushing product on people: "By the way, here are six bottles. Would you like six bottles?"

No. That is the worst. That is how you kill a luxury brand. Scarcity is the key, but it has to be true, authentic scarcity. You can't pretend.

Think about how most public tastings go. You go into a cool barn or room, they have a bunch of different wines, but they only pour the stuff they sell. They don't pour the good stuff. And even then, they only give you a little, tiny pour. Or worse, they charge you for the wine. And people wonder why they wasted their time.

Will you save money over the year on samples? Sure. But you don't make it up on sales. Give something to them. You want to build a high-end brand, you have to talk to people, connect with them, share with them. Ask what they like, tell them to check it out, and tell the story behind it. Don't sell them.

Don't say, "Here's our 2014. It pairs well with chicken." If someone says, "This goes with chicken," I think, "So does Sprite."

To me, branding and marketing comes through more face-to-face interactions, and it's not just my face. It's also seeing the staff face-to-face. Then, how do you translate that message and authenticity to them?

What happens is, a lot of times wineries will hire someone to give you the tour. Then they take you on that tour, and they don't really know how to tell the story—mainly because they haven't lived it, "This is winemaker so-and-so, and senior manager so-and-so." They're taught what to say, but they don't know it. Someone asks questions, and they just stare, blank-faced.

A number of years ago, my brother-in-law and I went over to a large Napa winery. We got a "special" tour. We went back and there was this big wall of barrels. Massive barrels everywhere. There was one barrel in the middle of the room. There's our barrel tasting. And I thought, "Really, dude?" We tasted out of a barrel, yes. But it was the barrel that everyone tastes wine out of, and it wasn't properly taken care of. This was not an actual barrel they aged wine in. What's in there? This was not an actual barrel tasting. They did this for a winemaker. They didn't know, and I didn't tell them who I was, but damn, man, what are you doing? That's not an authentic barrel tasting experience.

I dive in and bring people into the heart of what I do; people who have never experienced this before, because nobody does this. I bring people into my cellar, I let them see everything. Then, you get the right kind of people on your list. The ones who are groovy and cool. I show them, "OK, here's how to properly handle a barrel."

Then, every other experience they have at every other place, they compare to us and we come out looking way better.

You go to any other place and the tour ends with, "Oh, here's our wine club. We have a 10 percent off sale." They've got their little sales thing, and they've got it all orchestrated and dialed in. You can buy this today if you want. You have to go through some channels, but it's available right now.

People feel obligated to buy something if you push it on them, but I don't want people buying wine from me for that reason. I want people to buy because they love the wine, and they want to drink it and share it with their friends.

Look, this is a great way to sell wine. There's nothing wrong with that; it's cool. People will buy it all day long, so sell that way if you want. But it's not what I do. That's just me and I how I see it.

HOW I DO TOURS AND TASTINGS

First off, I can do exclusive tours and tastings because we are a direct-to-consumer focused model. When people come to visit my winery, I don't have to worry about anything other than the people on the list, and the people who want to be on the list. That makes it much easier to be exclusive and scarce.

Then, I only give tours and tastings to people on our list,

or people we have some connection to, or have some other reason to bring in. They have to call ahead and get an appointment, and we don't give those to just anyone. It has to be the right kind of people. Mainly because we don't have a lot of time, or enough wine.

I have to be choosy because I spend two to three hours with people, and I invest time in getting to know them and orchestrating a great tour for them. I can't do that for everyone.

Lemme break down how I run our tours, to show how seriously I take this:

When people come to a tasting, I'll ask if they have a driver. "Who's driving? You are? Cool. OK, you can smell the wine." I joke with them, lighten the mood, try to get a measure of who they are and what they are looking for, so I can tailor the tour to them.

I'll maneuver the story so they can latch onto it. Are they wine geeks? Do they just want to get drunk? Are they just here having fun?

When people come to the winery and I don't know them, I try to size them up when they arrive. It starts with their car. Do they have a chauffeur? Did they show up in a Bentley or a Mazda? Did they come in a bus? You name it.

Then, I look at their appearance. Are they laid-back, with a Tommy Bahama style, or are they geeked out in nerd gear? Are they overdressed or underdressed?

Then, when they come in, what are they like? What are they doing? Eye contact? Body language? Are they nervous, or relaxed? What's their attitude? It ranges from "Hell, what's going on" to "I am so stoked to be here" to "What have you got?" So, attitude is another clue on how to run the tour.

Then, you start a conversation. Why are they in town? A business trip? Wine trip? Then you start asking questions, and you can expand in any direction needed. "What are you guys into? What do you want to do?"

Some people just want to be guided and led through. I leave it open at the beginning, so they can try a variety of things. This is where I can really get into identifying and determining which bucket they fall into. They might want to see the barrels, hear about how one of the wines was made, talk about how they've been making some wine and want to learn more about the process.

You have people that come out here for the week to drink, or some do a girls' weekend and do some wine tasting for fun. They're just relaxing, having fun. They want to tell stupid stories and enjoy themselves.

Then, there's the crowd that's a bit older. They want to have fun, but they're more dialed in. They come to wineries because they already know something about wine.

You ask them what they like, what they have in their cellar, those kinds of questions. Then, you get the serious over-thinkers, you know? They want to show you that they know everything; when really, they don't know anything. So, I make them relax. I don't call them out on it.

Then, you've got the wine geek that arrives in a Mazda. Nothing wrong with that, they just typically don't have as high of an income. But they're geeked out on this stuff, in the best way. These guys will buy four bottles of this, sell two, and profit by selling half of their wine. They take the extra money and buy this, trade that. It's a game. They geek out over just one bottle, but they've got to buy four. They're passionate, and they are into it. It's one of the thoughts at the forefront of their minds. This is a very special group, and one I identify with.

I know a ton of them that come in. I always greet them, and we start geeking out on wine. They love it. Some of them really want to get technical, but some of them just want to get out of the basement and hang with other wine dudes, their favorite producers, or whatever, and taste some stuff. They get kind of weird about it (the tasting), but in a cool way. I get into that and I'm sincere about it, because I understand the animal and I'm one of them.

For everyone else, I base it on what they want. Another group are the partiers. They come in a limousine. A group of six to eight of them will show up. They're the ones that fall asleep with their face in the soup. But they are super fun. And if they found us, someone in their group knows wine and is connected, so someone in that group is a badass.

So, those are some different groups of people, and they're easy to identify. There's a story and a method of entertaining each one. I tell our hospitality people we aren't in the business of selling or marketing wine—we're in the entertainment business. We have a different medium to entertain people. If you can entertain people in a way that makes them want to watch your movie, read your book, or listen to your music, you can create an experience that makes them want to drink your wine.

People want to be entertained. They want to get a good product, they want to share it with their friends and family back in New Jersey, and hopefully they will all dig it.

After the small talk and I figure out which bucket they fall into and what they are looking for, I give them a little Chardonnay. Or maybe we get into bottles. But I make sure to get them some wine.

Then I do a quick general tour, unless they steer me hard in a certain direction. If they don't, I'll give them a brief overview of the equipment and what we do. I'll purposely go by places that are ordered and in line. (That's for the OCD in me, right?)

I want to show them the forklifts are all lined up; the pallet jacks and everything are lined up. I don't point it out, but I walk them by it. In that kind of an environment, everything has to be dialed in. You don't want to go to a winery that's in shambles and dirty. There's a mangy dog sitting there, and Uncle Fred is drunk on the patio—you don't want that. Maybe they won't pay attention to those things, but subconsciously, they see it. They see that my place is in order. So they unconsciously understand that if I have my place in order, I have my wine and my craft just as dialed in.

That's what we're doing here: making sure they know we're dialed in. I go around and show them what's going on, then get into more juicy things with the wine.

I take them through that whole circle, and then bring them through the lab. I show them fun stuff, and I'll ask them to find the ceramic gecko. I have a little gecko waiting in the corner. I got it in Hawaii. I do that to throw them off base, or to be a little whimsical.

Then if it's the right time of year, we go taste out of the tank, or do something that you don't typically see, feel, or touch, right? I love having people at harvest because they come in and the tanks are bubbling; I get excited because it's very cool. I say, "Come up here, man, check this out. This fermenter is almost done; see how the cap is sinking? Smell it—it has a certain smell.

"Now, this is just cold soaking, came off the vineyard yesterday. It's just fruit; smell that. Grab that, take ten berries and put them in your mouth." "Oh man, that tastes good." "Yeah, there's nothing in there but grapes, isn't that cool?"

Or if it's another time of year, I say, "I have a cool barrel over here. This is what this is...it's unique, and it will be blended out into something cool, but right now it's a single barrel." It's the truth, and you crawl way back and jump on a barrel, pull the bung, extract some wine, and then lean over and pour it into someone's glass.

Most people say they have never barrel tasted. I say, "Really? Check this out." And we barrel taste and we get into the wine.

They think, "Wow, that was kind of different." They think it was cool. It was real; you didn't make that up. These are real barrels and our real wine. Those little edges, right? People love that.

Then I'll say, "You want to hear some instruments? Check the bass tone on this." I'll do the music thing. I try to make sense to people. It's an experience. It's not like, "This came from this type of oak, and this certain clone, and we did whole cluster..." Shoot me in the head. Very few people care about that but winemakers, at least until they really get into wine.

I tell some fun stories about these places. I make it real, because it is. Let's talk to each other as people. Let's create something you'll remember and tell your friends, and hopefully you have an enjoyable experience.

Obviously this changes depending on the group. If I have partiers and drinkers, I gloss over the technical stuff, maybe skip the catwalk. They aren't as interested in the details—they just want to get to the wine. I make sure they have what they need, and that they don't go overboard. Then, we just start telling jokes and talking about the Old Country, stuff like that. And then we'll wind up on the patio relaxing, having a great day.

We get wine snobs, and I shorten those tours. They aren't the same as wine geeks, which I love. Wine snobs are "well-bred," and think they know a lot about wine, but really, they don't. I play up their ego when they come in. "Oh, really? Oh, I haven't had that one. Oh, that guy, really? You know him? That's great. Tell me more about you."

Those are the type that will spin you off topic because they just want to talk about themselves. "I met this dude and that dude, I got this and that..." They just want to tell me everything they know. They have a lack of confidence, or they're overcompensating for something. So you just play along, get through it. Wine snobs are the most tiresome group of people. But honestly, they are great customers, and once I get them past the bragging, they can be pretty cool. It's all about being real, and they get it eventually.

The trophy hunters are another group that likes wine. They are the ones who want the highest rated, most exclusive wines. They spend a lot of money on it, buy a ton of wine. I'm down with that. But they don't know anything about wine, and they don't care to know anything about it—it's just a status symbol. But they tend to be upfront about their lack of knowledge, which is cool. Honesty is endearing. Knock yourself out, man.

Then you get some people who are seriously high-end, cool, successful people, and they're the most humble. They know what they like. They appreciate wine and they have a similar sort of vibe—they're more real. They have a lot of stuff going on, but they enjoy wine, and they're seeking out things they enjoy in life, rather than seeking out things to impress their buddies or other people. They are a distinct crowd, even though some of them might run in the same circles as the other groups. They've finally arrived at a place where they are seeking experiences rather than status. Very cool.

No matter the group, I hope they enjoy the wine. I want them to think it was interesting. I want to see their body language, and if they connect with the story. It's mainly in their body language—that's what gives it away. Is this working? If something isn't resonating, I ask different questions or go a different route to get an answer. It depends on the group. If they know wine, I can ask, "What do you think? How is it?" If they don't know wine, I'll say other things, like, "These grapes have this certain characteristic. The mouthfeel comes around to be this." Then I'll see if they caught the comment, and if they actually experienced and tasted what I described.

Not everyone will like everything I pour, and that's OK. But if I can help them understand what they are tasting, and how it fits with other wines, then they can learn something and get it. They can actually understand more what they do like, and why. It opens their minds to what's behind a wine, and how a wine was built, rather than the context of a finished wine.

People will tell you what they think. You just listen. I've always been the kind of guy who will say it: either you like something, or you don't. Some people don't like our wine, and that's OK. Not everybody is going to like it, but for the people who do, we want to make the wines good for them.

People will tell me they had a bottle of our wine, and they

liked it. No one really says, "Hey, I had a bottle of your wine, and it sucked." But I still want to get feedback. I just try to be inquisitive and find out how people really feel about it. Not what they're saying, but what they're really feeling—what they're saying without words.

And to be honest, I like it when people say they don't like our wine, because then I can ask them what they don't like. And maybe they don't like our style, or maybe I made a mistake with the wine. I will make changes based on feedback, if I think it's on point. Or I won't do a thing.

For example, someone has a glass of wine. You pour them something and they say, "Yeah, cool," and they move it away. They're saying, "That wasn't good, dude. Why'd you pour that for me?" Or, it could be the complete opposite: "Wow, now I'm interested. I'm going to lay back and study this a bit."

They're not thinking about studying it; they're just studying it. They're going, "Cool, tell me more about this." So that's how you noodle information out of people—kind of in that manner. Watching them. Do they really like it, or are they just saying that to be polite? Most people aren't thinking about this, but you can tell what they are thinking if you watch and listen.

It's not really different than what we did originally at John

Ash, and I still do that on tours. It's important information. Sometimes, we'll have a wine that may be a little off style. I don't ask them directly, "Is this working?" Tours and tastings are a constant study of consumers for me. I am always trying to get better, and in wine, getting better is ultimately about making wine that people love.

The coolest thing is at the end of our tours, I might give them a bottle of wine, if they're cool and I think they will enjoy it and understand why they are getting it. I ask, "Where are you having dinner? Here you go. Drink it now, later, whatever. Thanks for coming."

After I give them wine and they ask about buying more, I say, "Yeah, about that. Typically it's two to three years to get on our list, but I might be able to move you up, depending on the vintage. Here's the deal. I can probably get you on a bit earlier, but no guarantees. We just don't have the wine right now."

That is true—I like to hook up the people who come in, if I can. But demand far exceeds supply, so it's difficult.

Then, they're like, "You just spent three hours with me, and you're not going to sell me anything? This is just free? What the hell?" They walk out thinking, "What just happened?"

They talk about the experience with their friends. And

they respect you and like you and like the wine even more, because now they have a cool story to tell about it.

It's like getting behind-the-scenes access. But you have to wait for the final show. It's about authenticity. What we're building here, you can't fake.

OUR EMOTIONAL CONNECTION TO WINE

I know I just dove into the details a lot, but let me zoom back out and tell you a story that might help you see how it all loops around and connects.

We have a customer, a seventy-five-year-old guy named Jerry Williams. He's been with us forever. And he would call me every offering.

Jerry: "Michael, it's Jerry Williams. My allocation went down again. It's only three bottles."

Michael: "Jerry, you know the game. We do this every year. You get the same as what you ordered last year, and you ordered three bottles last year."

Jerry: "I know, but I used to get twelve."

Michael: "I'll get you what you want, Jerry. Just tell me, and I can up your allocation."

Jerry: "Well, I only want two bottles this year."

I had to laugh. He wasn't complaining. He just wanted to talk. That's cool, I love that, he's a good dude, been with us forever.

Well, one day I got an email from one of his family members telling me he passed away. He was buried with full military honors.

It was a big ceremony. They told me he was buried in a Steelers jersey, with a Cubs baseball bat, and a bottle of Kosta Browne.

He was buried with a bottle of KB. 2008, Garys' Vineyard to be exact.

I was truly humbled. I couldn't believe that something we did touched somebody in a way that he wanted to buried with a bottle of our wine. It meant that much to him. And it meant even more to me.

That tells me that if you're open to it, wine can touch your soul.

There's something magical about wine. It's been around for so long, and it's been done pretty much in the same way for as long as civilization has existed. There's something about the fermentation and the romanticism about it—the land connection to it. Whether we know it or not, we're all connected to the land.

Wine also slows people down. You've had a hectic, busy day. You hit dinner and you're still on edge. The wine relaxes you, slows you down, and hopefully the conversation gets interesting.

Or, hopefully it helps you connect to other people. It connects people to things that they wouldn't typically be connected to in their daily lives.

Wine is somewhat ceremonial, as well. You get the bottle out of your cellar and tell the story about where you got it, the story behind it. It's not a huge ceremony, but it is ceremonial.

Wine is like the fluid of connection between people.

I can't tell you how many times I'll hear things like:

"We wanted to let you know we shared this wine we got from you with my dad. It was the last wine he ever had before he passed."

"We were saving this bottle for our anniversary, and when we drank it, it brought back memories of when we came to your winery."

It blows my mind because I feel like we're just making freaking wine and trying to do the best we can to serve our customers. But it touches people in so many ways beyond just drinking fermented grape juice.

I got into wine because I had similar experiences of my own. These customer experiences don't shock me—they're just humbling.

Wine is greater than any person, in a sense. It's been around for thousands of years, and it will be around for another thousand years. Wine is a part of cultures all around the world.

There's no confirmed written history of humans that doesn't include wine. Jesus turned water into wine 2,000 years ago. When Baptists tell me they don't drink, I tell them that Jesus drank wine. He's had a stressful day, rising from the dead, man. He needs a glass of wine.

I don't want to get crazy here. We aren't saving the world. But that's OK. In fact, maybe the world doesn't need saving. Maybe what we need is to talk to each other more, to connect and understand each other. And if wine helps us sit down and talk, and make those conversations a little better, that's enough for me.

CHAPTER 9

THE NAYSAYERS

THROUGHOUT THIS PROCESS OF BUILDING A WINE company, I've learned that I can't be an open book.

It's not a personal thing—it's more part of the business strategy. I don't really feel like people have ever taken advantage of me personally.

But, if you give a little, show a little weakness, or show authenticity over your story, there are people out there that will take bits of that and try to use it to break you down. They'll do it in front of other people, because some people talk trash. Gossipers.

They talk about what we do at the winery. Why aren't you going to this event, why are you hanging out with this person, or why aren't you hanging out with that person?

It's just normal social stuff, I guess, but it seems to be petty and silly.

For example, there are other wineries that make assumptions about what we do and where we came from. They'll say, "Oh, those guys. They just have it made, and they do whatever they want. They didn't work for it. They just got lucky." They say stuff like that.

I always think, "What are you talking about? You know what we did to succeed; you saw us do it."

On the surface, I hear about this stuff all the time. We don't do that to anyone else, but we hear it.

I hear what some people think about how we make our wine. They'll say we pick our stems out, dry them out, and then put them back in. They'll say something like, "I knew a guy who was roommates with an intern at the winery, and he told me all about how they do it."

I mean, come on. Really?

Or they say we add this or that to the wine. We add this component, or all that component, or whatever. There's no way to make that wine without using this, they'll say. They can't get these textures and quality without manipulating it, we hear.

What? No, really, it's just grapes.

People have said that we lie about the allocation models. Nobody can do that. Yeah, you can mislead somebody at a cocktail party, but you can't lie about fundamentals. Everyone knows.

We've had our share of haters—I guess anyone successful does. It's not unique to us at all.

I should just let it all flow off my back, but I'm human, you know. It's made me more guarded.

People see where we are today, but they don't know where we came from and how hard it was. They want to leapfrog and have it easy. They say, "It only took him four years." Yeah, that's what you think. Good luck doing this in four years. Try twenty.

And then people get confused when I tell them how it really went down, and how many years this took, and how hard it was.

It's funny, this friend of mine, one time he says, "Man, every year, you guys are still going. Your momentum is still growing. What are you guys doing so right? Everyone's pissed about it."

He was kind of joking, but it's true, you know? People have a hard time accepting it.

I mean, what do you want from me here? Make better wine, and market it better. It is simple to understand. It's just hard to do.

I honestly don't know why people hate people who succeed. Not even just on us; why they hate on anyone at all. What does it get you? How do you benefit?

The only thing I can see is that it helps people feel better about their own lack of success, or their own choices that have led to bad consequences. When you try and fail, or when you are too scared to even try, maybe it makes you feel better to talk trash about other people.

I don't know. It's hard for me to understand. I've tried and failed so many times; you've read about it in this book. But I just kept going and focused on what I was doing, not others.

I will say this: we make a conscious effort to be great.

What I tell our staff is that it's so easy to be good. With the soil and the environment and the grapes in our area, you can lie down on your laurels and you're good.

To be great is harder.

Being exceptional, it's kind of edgy. It requires so much attention to detail. So much more effort.

The amount of effort it takes to be good is a lot. And then to be great, it takes exponentially more. Now, if you want to exceptional, it takes more than what it took for good and great combined. And if you want to be the very best? That's even MORE effort.

This is why most people stop at good, or even great. They don't want to put in the work. It's so much harder to reach the highest levels.

To be the best.

There's no reason in the world you can't try. The only thing stopping you is a lack of willingness, dedication, and balance. It's a decision you have to make.

That's where I try to go.

I may make it or I may not, but I'm going to do everything I can in my power to get there.

And there's no room up there for hate.

CHAPTER 10

A BIT ABOUT THE WINE BUSINESS

I GET A LOT OF QUESTIONS FROM A LOT OF PEOPLE who want to get into wine. Whether it's young people who want to break into the business, or very successful people who want to start their own vineyard and winery business, or any number of other types.

I decided to put this section together to try and collect some of what I think about this subject.

I don't want to make it seem like this is the ultimate word on how and why to get into wine. It's not. It's just my perspective from twenty years in this business.

STARTING YOUR OWN WINERY

I try to persuade people not to get into the wine business all the time. I mean, almost every week, it seems like.

I'm not talking about a young kid who is super into winemaking and farming and loves making wine. No, that's cool if that's your thing. I will always encourage those people if they really love the craft. If growing grapes and working in wine is your dream, go for it—you can definitely make it happen.

Here's what I am talking about: I meet someone who has made it in whatever industry, and they've got some money in the bank. They see what we have, they see the vineyards and they see the front of the deal. They see the romantic part. And they want that part.

They tell me they have been very successful in their career or previous career, and they love the romantic side of it, and they want their own winery. It looks cool, their friends will think it's cool, and they think they can buy the same thing.

They ask, "Should I buy this? It's a nice house and it has ten acres of grapes—it looks really great. I think I could make good wine there."

I tell them if they buy it, they should lease out the vineyard. Don't be a part of it. They won't make any money off that.

Lease the vineyard to a winery and just enjoy the view and make a little money off of it. The conversation goes like this:

Person: "Yeah, but if we keep the grapes, then I can make some wine of my own."

Michael: "You know what a sailboat is?"

Person: "Yeah."

Michael: "It's something you dump your money into, right?"

Person: "Right."

Michael: "You know what a vineyard is? It's something you dump your sailboats into."

Or, I'll reverse it on them. If, for example, I'm talking to a high-powered attorney that wants to be a winemaker, I'll say something like:

Michael: "Oh yeah, I know what you mean about wanting to get into wine. I've been wanting to practice law. It can't be that hard. I'll get a good law consultant like you to help me out when I go to trial. My dream is to have a big trial in New York City, where I nail a freaking mobster, just like Rudy Giuliani!"

Attorney: "Are you high? That's impossible!"

You laugh, but it's the same thing. Wine is just as complex and nuanced, especially the business of wine.

You have to take the wine business super seriously: you need to spend a lot of time learning everything about it, because it has the great potential of taking a significant amount of funds from your bank account and then some. There will be a great deal of wine to drink, though.

These people come to wine at that point in their life after they've done something completely different. And they think that business is business, no matter what it is. Yes, there are fundamentals of business and many of them are similar to the wine business, but the wine business is different. Even the banking is different—there's a completely different set of bankers that deal with wine because it's so out there. They have to use different strategies. The economics of it are different. Most aspects about wine are different; that might be why I'm so into it...because it is different.

And don't think just because you're parked next to some hot winery that you will be the same. I hear that all the time. "We've got this property next to the Best Winery in Napa." OK, that's good. Lots of people are next to them. But their wine sells for half the price, and they have four vintages in the warehouse. How does that impact your financial modeling?

Wine is a long-term play, no matter how you look at it. It is a game of patience. People want to leapfrog ahead, but they've only done it for so long, and poof, they're gone. I've never seen anyone leapfrog their way to success in this business. It took us ten years to get to our breakthrough moment, and that's considered fast for this industry. Plus, it was a lot of work to get there. So much that I am surprised I survived the journey.

If you want to have a pretty vineyard in your front yard, go for it, just lease it out. If you want to make wine, just do a little bit. Do a barrel, put it in your cellar. You've got your barrel of wine. Your friends might want to taste it. It's cool, and it's a fun hobby. Go for it.

I persuade people against it a lot. I don't want to, but it's mainly because I don't want them to be disappointed. People get upset at me because they think I'm trying to crush their dreams, but I'm not. I don't want them to lose their passion for wine in the process of trying to be a wine producer.

I've seen it happen so many times. Someone gets into it with lots of money and the best intentions, and ten years later, everything sucks.

I remember one guy specifically. I tried to tell him; he didn't want to listen. Ten years later he told me, "I'm going to sell my property. All I wanted to do was sit on my porch and work on my vineyard. Then we decided to start making wine, and now we're selling wine, and I hate it. I hate it. My whole love for wine is gone. I want to move out of the state. This is bad."

They lost quite a bit on their wine project.

Most people's passion is not a *passion for the process of making wine*. They have a passion for something that comes from the process. They fell in love with an experience they had with wine, not making the wine, which is very different. But if you want to have a successful winery, you need to love the process, not just the result.

I told you my story already. I walked into the Silver Oak barrel room and knew I was going to do this. I wanted to be a craftsman and businessman, and I knew that day that wine would be my canvas. I think most wine people have an experience like this. I don't think those people get into the wine business to make money. There is a way to make money in the wine industry, but people get into it because they're passionate about the craft. That's where it starts. They want to make it their profession. Their lifestyle.

And some people new to the industry actually get that, put their boots on, and get dirty. Go through it with respect to the vines and the craft. They start small, take their time, and above all, they respect Mother Nature and all that she brings. And maybe make some good wine and sell it so they can continue in the business. Now that is cool!

AN INTERESTING MINDSET FOR WINEMAKERS

I meet a lot of young winemakers. Some of them are making killer wines, and make me very optimistic for the future. But man, some of them are lost.

There are two major problems that young people in wine have:

1. They just blindly follow everyone else and don't think for themselves, or
2. They want to reinvent everything.

Both of these approaches are wrong, in my opinion.

If you want to make wine, that is awesome. Let me make something very clear first: humans have been making wine for over 5,000 years. The oldest known winery was found in Armenia. More specifically, in the Areni-1 cave in Vayots Dzor, which was dated to c. 4100 BC. Those are some deep roots. You're better off starting by studying the craft of wine-making and proper farming techniques. You aren't going to reinvent anything. You may be part of innovation, which is very important and relevant to the ongoing pursuit of the craft and farming, but reinvention is something that cannot be done. Well, it may be attempted, but I'm not sure if I would like to drink the wines.

I see young people come in and want to build a better mousetrap, make their mark, and do all these new things. I was one of those but got humbled very early. Not by people, but by Mother Nature and her force. They want to try different farming practices that make no sense. Or they'll see a vineyard in Burgundy doing something in a certain way, and say we should do it here. Well, we're in completely different environments, so study that first and then decide on what vineyard practices may be the best for a particular region and more specifically, for a certain place (piece of dirt). Some aspects from the motherland may be relevant, just be careful.

I am not talking about blindly following rules or practices just because they are rules. It's not that at all. I am all about breaking those rules if there are certain things that may be new or may not be what has always been done. You can break all of the "rules" that you want and I'll cheer you on, or I may be skeptical, but that is only one view from one person. I am talking about Mother Nature and what she brings to the place, vine, and ultimately the grape. When you start trying to mess with Mother Nature, that is a fight you cannot win (I talk about this more below).

Some people will think they'll make some wine from a terroir that just won't allow it. For example, this is a big thing with Pinot, the low alcohol/high alcohol debate. This debate has been and still is not only a hot topic for some, but really does not have the merit that quite a few people base the theory on. Most aspects in fine wine have to fall in line with the terroir, for the most part. So, they say, "I'm gonna make a lean wine, and it will be like Burgundy because I'm picking at twenty-two brix."

Do you like eating underripe peaches? I don't. I like eating a perfectly ripened peach picked from the tree at the right moment. Not even the right day, but the right moment. If the peaches are picked too early, the peach pie that you are putting so much into will lack flavor and balance. You can have everything else right in the pie but if the fruit is not up to what it could be, the pie will not be able to generate the senses in the way that is possible. Same thing is true for wine. If the grapes are not up to the best potential flavor, the wine will lack something in most cases. On the flip side, picking overripened grapes will potentially lead to a dense and perhaps a monolithic wine. Just my perspective.

Some of these people want to make their mark, but they follow other people to do it, instead of thinking for themselves.

You want to be a good winemaker? Don't follow people too closely, and don't try and reinvent the wheel. Don't get me wrong. I encourage people to study what other winemakers and farmers do and to get as many mentors as you can. Lots of great teachers out there. And then use this knowledge and make your own style. Be true to what you like—it has to be what you like. If you like insipid, anorexic wines, then go for it; but just make sure you have enough consumers so you can stay in business. You can say the same thing with big, overripe wines. If you have enough consumers to buy it, God bless you. And again, do your best to make a style that you like, whatever that may be.

Calm down. Study the craft. Work very hard. That's what I tell the young people. "Study, study, study. Work, work, work. Pedigree, pedigree, pedigree, and then ride off into the sunset in a cool way." It takes time to get your stuff dialed in. Wine is a business of patience.

I'm not saying don't be different; I'm just saying don't swing so far out of the realm that nobody will get it. People do that because they're chasing after something they think is cool, and they're trying to impress wine snobs or reviewers, instead of worrying about actual people who buy wine.

The extremes are "I'm going to be totally obscure" or "I'm going to be totally like everybody else and have no personality."

The middle is the road to take: "Be authentic to who you are, to the vineyard, and what the terroir is."

Learn the vineyard; learn the best farming methods for that vineyard. Make sure you have someone tending the vineyard well, if it's not you. Study your craft to make sure that when you get the grapes, you know what to do with them. Style them in a way that makes sense to you. Hopefully, if that works and you have a sensible palate on you, you'll have enough consumers to buy your wine.

MOTHER NATURE

People will ask me, "How's the vintage?" and I laugh, "I'll tell you when we pick the grapes."

You can have 364 days that are exactly the same with a great vintage. Then, you have one day of hail or something else Mother Nature throws at you, and it messes it up. But that's what I like about it; it's unpredictable. I love the differences in vintages. It is Mother Nature's signature for that season. It would drive most people nuts, but I embrace it. I like it. It doesn't keep me up at night or anything.

OK, Mother Nature, I respect you. I will bow down. It's so cool and humbling, because Mother Nature is the key to life.

As far as time goes, we're lucky enough to be here at a certain point in time, when cultivation and farming have progressed to the right place. There's no forcing any of this stuff. You have to ride with her, be respectful, and enjoy her.

"Sorry it rained so much" or "Sorry there's no rain." It's a cycle, and you deal with it. So, when a forecast comes up, no matter what it is, we know we'll get through it. We've been through heat, rain, cold, and hail, whatever.

You build on it, and it's funny to talk to the old-timers. They'll say, "I haven't seen a vintage like this. It is kind of like this, but we did this, and it didn't work. You might try this, but that might not work. We tried this or that and it worked beautifully. There's a new trellising system you might want to try; it's a new thing, but I don't know. We tried this other thing, but it's not going to work. I don't need to see it; I heard about it, and I know it's not going to work. We're going to stick to doing things this way—it might be the right way, or maybe we're just stubborn."

The message is that you'll never figure it all out. It's impossible. There is too much to know. Mother Nature is too complex to control.

I talked to this guy, Fred Scherrer of Scherrer Winery. He's an amazing grower and winemaker, a very smart person. He grew up on a vineyard in Alexander Valley and owns his own winery. He's a cool cat, and a great musician. I was beating my head against a wall trying to figure out a problem, so I asked him about it.

I said, "Fred, you grew up on a vineyard. You've been making wine your whole life. When did you figure this out, because I'm having a hard time wrapping my head around it."

He said, "Michael, I've come to understand that it takes two consecutive adult lifetimes to figure this out."

I think he's right. Then, I'm down in Australia for a Pinot conference. The night we arrived, we went to someone's house for dinner—party of ten. Aubert de Villaine was there, the owner of Domaine de la Romanée-Conti. Aubert was at the head of the table, and I was sitting next to him. I turned my chair to him to engage in conversation, and started the conversation with a similar question I asked Fred:

"You've been doing this for a long time—your dad, your granddad. You have all these grand cru vineyards, you know the dirt and soil, and you make incredible wines. You must feel so comfortable with your process and place. What are you doing that other people aren't?"

He replied, "No, Michael. I try to understand it, and we try to make better wine, but it's just elusive and ever-changing."

I found great comfort in that.

The next day, there were three hundred people at this conference, and everyone wanted his attention. I just wanted to thank him for the great conversation and say, "See you later." I wasn't going to bug the guy. He was talking to a wine importer, and I said, "Mr. de Villaine, I just want to say thank you for the conversation last night."

He says, "Oh, Michael," and pulls out a yellow pad of paper and says, "I went back to my room and wrote down notes. Just focus on this."

He said, "Focus on the vineyards. Focus on what the grapes are telling you and what the place is telling you. Don't try to manipulate the wines or overwork the wines. Let them be what they are. Respect the terroir."

Here I was talking to Aubert de Villaine, possibly the greatest Pinot Noir winemaker in the world, and he is trying to work through the issues like I was, just at a different level, with a greater understanding. Yeah, he's further ahead than I was, but still, we're walking the same path. Incredibly humbling and valuable experience in many ways.

Humble people keep learning—arrogant people stop learning. The wisest old men realize they know nothing. I live by that, and it's true, man. Every time I start to think I know how to make wine, something happens and I realize I know very little.

You have to be open to learning. You have to be open to new ideas and also respect the history, and you have to stay out of your own way sometimes too. All of these things.

I like to be out in nature. It's very calming. I'm comfortable because something is in control, and it's balanced; it's been doing that for millions of years. Watching things grow amazes me—like grapes. Year after year, they keep putting out fruit. Where does it all come from? Scientifically, you can explain it, but there's more to it. How do they propagate, and how did they evolve to that point? How do they adapt to the environment and be so strong?

We're intimately involved in it, and the product we make comes from the earth; we simply transform it through fermentation. Fermentation is also a natural process. You drop grapes on the ground, they will ferment. That's how things are done. It's a fertilizer—it literally makes the ground more fertile.

In all of history, in all the countries of the world, what do we brag about? "We have the best cheese, bread, beer, and wine." All fermented products.

I love to look out into our backyard. I love the morning I open up the blinds, and we've got plants, trees, flowers, and wildlife everywhere. I go outside, do my stretches, walk around, smell the air, and watch the foxes run by. Mother Nature is right there.

I think those that are close to the vineyard engage with Mother Nature quite a bit, as well as those who are more spiritual about their craft—those who are into it because they love it.

There's also a lot that goes into the scientific approach. We do this for this reason; this is going to happen because of that. We're going to add this and do that, and then we'll get a good crop, right? It's more mechanical than it is nature.

There's a crowd that really gets into the natural vibe of things—the ebb and flow of it. They have a respect for the earth, the craft, what it really means, how to make something, and hold true to where it comes from. Then, add elements and coax it along to finalize it, like the sound of a guitar. There is also a sense of health in a vineyard. It's much more than the vines; it's everything that is in the vineyard and is around the vineyard. That is the terroir.

I think all the elites in the wine business, you pick the highest end producer, they're all connected on this level. I don't think they can plan it or measure it, or use only rational reasons. I don't think you can express it. It's like a good jam session with the right people. It comes from a lot of experience.

HARVESTING THE GRAPES

One of the questions I get the most from people, mostly wine people but not always, is about harvest.

Before I talk about that, lemme tell you a story.

When I was a kid, we'd walk to this one peach orchard. There weren't a lot of peaches where I lived, and I loved peaches.

In the summertime, we'd go to this peach orchard and eat peaches for lunch. One day, there was this peach hanging from the tree, right in the sun. It was warming in the sun, and warm to the touch. I picked it, and it just fell into my hand. I didn't really need to pick it; it was perfectly ripe, at that moment.

It was a beautiful peach. I smelled it—it had an aromatic perfume. I took a bite, and had juice running down my arm. The flavor of the peach exploded in my mouth. It was perfectly tree ripened. I'd never had a peach like that, and the memory of it seared a sensory experience in my mind that stuck with me my whole life.

That's what I go on for grapes. That experience kind of cemented that—I pick grapes based on flavor.

Yeah, you have to use some chemistry, but I pick on flavor. There are a lot of different factors, but that's the main thing, for sure. It's fruit juice. It should taste good.

I don't harvest when the grapes are falling off, or when

they're too tight and green. Basically, that means overripe and underripe. In most vintages, over time, the middle part starts to break down a little bit and becomes mealy, and the skins get a little crunchy. When you bite into them, they're almost crisp; the flavors pop. For me, it's all about having the flavors pop.

Every vintage is different, so the timing on this varies depending on that. But there are usually about three days to harvest while they still have good integrity, and the flavors are there. That's when you want to pick.

I taste all the grapes. The only way to truly know when to pick the grapes is to be in vineyards and taste the grapes constantly.

Then you've got to watch the skies. What's the weather pattern doing? How's the canopy management out there? Can it withstand some heat? Is there any mold or mildew pressure out there? If it rains, how much will it rain? Can the tractors get in there?

We do look at the sugar level (brix), but we don't pay too much attention to it for a picking decision. It's all about flavors. If it's a late season, we focus on pH level. Once the pH starts rising, it means the vines are shutting down, and you won't get much else out of them. We look at brix, pH, total acidity; they're all indicators and useful tools.

We don't have a specific formula on chemistry for making a picking decision. Some people will say, "We're picking at a 23.5 brix, no matter what." Or, "I'm going to pick at 3.4 pH, no matter what." OK, go for it. It could be earlier or later, unless you're tasting all the time and seeing what style you like.

People think that picking decisions are controversial because everyone has their own style and different ways of doing things. "This is how you should pick grapes." "No, this is how you should pick grapes." I say, pick them however you want—this is how I'm doing it. It's a very personal decision.

It's an involved process, but to me, it's about a flavor. It's fermented grape juice, and the better the grape tastes, the better the wine is going to taste.

ATTENTION TO DETAIL

This section is pretty intense wine knowledge. If you are a casual reader, you might want to skip it, but if you're a wine nerd like me, you might like it.

Another thing people miss is attention to detail. We work with the growers—they do the work in the vineyards, but we check in on what they're doing if need be. Not to scrutinize, but to get on the same page. Some of them know how to do it, and with others, it's important to stay involved in what we want and how we want it done. Everyone I have encountered in the grower realm wants to do the right thing, although everyone has a different point of view. It's like if you give five chefs a chicken and a few of the same ingredients, they will all make a different dish. Very similar to every other aspect of life.

We may think we have a better way of doing things, but sometimes not. The owners of these vineyards and the management teams that are involved vary in style of management. It is very personal for everyone involved. And I love that aspect of the sites and the growers that we deal with. I cannot emphasize the importance of individuality in each site. It is beyond important. Actually, it has the potential to reach the soul.

Our vineyard is our vineyard, and we deal with it how it makes sense to us. Our grower partners have the same sense of individuality, although they may have a different approach. It could be philosophical, technical, or logically driven. Or it could be that they know the site better than we may. We may also have some knowledge that they may not have. Both points of view are very valid, and that needs to be respected. Right along with the respect to Mother Nature.

When it comes to farming practices, timing is of the essence. A viticulturist manages the vines in every aspect throughout the year, and we work with them along the way. Understanding the soil and when to spray what, with the least amount of intrusion and with the most sustainable products that are effective.

Pruning is a very important part of the growing process. During winter, the vines go dormant with the previous season's growth still there. Very much like a rose bush. We all look at things down to the bud level, even smaller than my finger. There are hundreds of thousands of them. You have to pick the right one, and if you pick the right one, that might be your shoot for next year, or the following year. It is seriously intense and detailed work, but if you want great wine, that is how you have to do it.

Canopy management is crucial and comes with many logistical challenges. Basically, the canopy (shoots that grow vertically and hold all of the leaves) need to be managed at many stages of vine development during the season. Mainly for what the vines need but also for how we can get ahead of the work. The leaves are solar panels for the fruit. Photosynthesis. Too many leaves, the fruit gets blown out by too much power. Too few leaves, the fruit cannot ripen.

If we get behind, then we have major catching up to do. We need to get ahead of all of this so we don't later go in and have to rip apart the vines to get the shoots in the proper place for sunlight and air movement. Serious headache if we fall behind, both for us and also for the vines. Whenever vines are worked on, they feel it and will react in a certain way. The vines react to aggressive work on them with a reaction that sometimes can be detrimental. These are living, breathing plants that don't like aggression, so if we get in there gently, and do gentle work, they are happier. Just the way that it works.

We have some great growers. Koplen Vineyard is one example. Dennis Koplen and his wife, Lynn, do most of the work themselves. He's out there right now, I'm sure. Seven days a week. I went out a couple of days ago, and a guy working for Dennis says, "Hey, I got this all dialed in, I got all these leaves positioned." Dennis says, "No, you didn't." Dennis goes over there and pulls one leaf.

I'm serious. He and Lynn are that detailed.

You really want to look at vineyards during harvest time because that's when everything is dialed in. Sometimes you'll let stuff grow and get a little mangled through the growing season because you want to expend some energy and it looks a little funky, then you go and tighten it up. Sometimes a vineyard will look weird because of the state it's in, or it could look out of shape because the owner doesn't care or have the time to deal with it. Very complex situation.

One of our main growers and vineyard managers is Charlie Chenoweth. His attention to detail is off the hook. He manages our estate vineyard for Cirq. He has his way of doing things and it is always very precise. Intuition is key as well as listening to Mother Nature. Charlie is very well versed on both of these aspects. Very rare indeed. If you ever have the chance to dive into a conversation about grape growing with Charlie, I highly encourage you to do so.

There is also another aspect of vine management, which is logistics. We could, for example, have a wet part of the year. Rain. If that is the case, you have to wait until the soil dries out to get tractors in. It can also be difficult if there is a season when the vines really start growing quickly. There are only so many people who are trained properly to do the job, and there are a lot of vineyards that need tending. Also at harvest. If we have a rush to get the fruit off of the vine for some reason (heat or rain, for example), we need to get ahead of it to make sure we have the crews lined up and that they are available. Tricky stuff, although we have a system in place in regard to timing that we can implement when we see the situation getting a bit tight. I have had experiences when I was not on top of this, and things did not turn out so well. Every year we learn something new about this. The point is to learn from prior seasons but not let prior seasons dictate what a current season will be. Agility is key.

You have to pay very high attention to detail in the vineyard, especially with Pinot Noir. If one thing goes wrong, potentially everything can go wrong.

For example, you think you have a perfect vintage, every-thing is dialed in, and then you get a weather report that a heat wave is coming, so you have to pick at two in the afternoon, when it's 100 degrees outside. You have super hot fruit coming in, and you have to cool it down. It breaks the skin membranes, and starts taking off with fermentation. Your wine's not going to be as good, and that can happen. This is unacceptable, and we make sure that this does not happen. You want to avoid those things. To avoid this, we pick our fruit at night, starting around one or two in the morning. That is when the grapes have had a chance to cool off. Typically right around 50 degrees Fahrenheit. This is a crucial aspect of harvesting wine grapes. I cannot overem-phasize the importance of this enough at the high-end level.

Also, we have usually used half-ton bins to pick our grapes into. Pretty typical at this point in time for high-end grapes. With that size of a bin, the grapes tend to get compressed and start to juice. So, we are now working with small picking lugs. A lug is like a rectangular bucket, small. You know, like a bus tub. They hold about 30 pounds compared to 1,000 pounds in a bin. The grape clusters come to the winery intact.

To use these is a logistical challenge. Rather than having twenty, half-ton bins, we have hundreds of small lugs. We are willing to pay the extra cost since we get the grapes intact and ready for the sorting process respectfully. All of this time during the year to farm the vines and the grapes at the highest end, then we are going to compress them and disrespect them? I don't think so. Another thing that is unacceptable.

Logistically speaking, we bring these small containers to the vineyard on pallets. They are then sent out into the vineyard so the pickers have them at the ready. Very challenging but doable. Once filled, they are stacked once again on pallets full of grapes. They stack those up, and it comes into the winery in these protected bins. It's much more labor-intensive, but the fruit's more intact. We're doing it because of that. So many countless hours are spent on tending the vines and the clusters of beautiful fruit. Why ruin it at the end? This poses challenges due to the extra labor needed and the logistics that ensue. It is worth it, though. When we receive these clusters intact and with high-end integrity, the wine is better. Just the way it is.

When the fruit comes to the door, we immediately start the process. We call it a "sorting system." It comes to the door; you weigh it and get going on processing. If we are backed up for any reason, we put them in the cold room. We put them in a cold room to make sure the grapes stay cold—it's basically a refrigerator. Then, when we're ready to process, we do so. Sometimes it goes right to the line; sometimes it has to wait a bit.

Next, we'll hit the sorting line, and we do it by hand with

a few tools and pieces of equipment to help along the way. We hand sort all clusters at the start of the process. We do the best we can in the vineyard to ensure all clusters that are picked are of the best quality. As a quality check, we look at everything on the sorting table. We may have some overripe or underripe clusters, or perhaps some sort of mold or mildew issues. Happens from time to time, depending on the vintage. This is pretty labor intensive and takes quite a few hours on some days, twelve to fourteen hours and beyond at times. A bit intense doing the same thing for so many hours, but it is worth it.

Directly after that, the grapes go up to the destemmer if we are destemming the fruit. If not, we will do "whole cluster," which means we leave the grapes on the stems. It adds a certain nuance and character if done right in the right vintage. It varies every vintage. After the grapes are destemmed, they go through a delicate mechanical system that takes out anything we don't want. Mainly small, underdeveloped grapes or any small raisins that dried up early in the growing season. Pinot Noir has a tendency of doing this in certain years. What comes out is what we call caviar. The berries look like small, dark-colored blueberries with nothing else in the mix. Beautiful sight to be seen.

Harvest is an intense time. When it hits the fan, there are all kinds of things going on. In the heat of it, you have grapes coming in on one end, wine going in barrels on the other end, and everything in between. Press cycles, punch-downs, chemistry analysis, and all this different stuff. Barrel movements, barrel washings, I mean, there's a lot going on, and you have to orchestrate it all.

The clusters come in cold and need to come in cold. That's why we harvest at night; you want it right around 50 degrees. That's about ambient temperature at night where we are, so you want to maintain that. We put it in a vessel, whether it's a stainless-steel tank, a wood tank, or a concrete tank. Sometimes into small fermenters, one-ton capacity or so. It's all orchestrated based on what we want it to be, and then we figure out the space we have available.

Once the grapes are in the fermenter, we let them sit at 50 degrees Fahrenheit for four or five days. This is referred to as a "cold soak." During that time, we'll spread it with dry ice on top to keep the oxygen off. We don't want oxygen during that time because the bacteria are aerobic, which means they need air. They'll populate, and then the primary fermentation will cut that back. But then you will have a high population of bacteria, which can pose risks later on. There are ways to deal with that, but from my experience, it may take away from the nuance of a wine.

You keep the air off it, and then we inoculate it because it's under control. We do wild fermentation with the yeast, but if it just takes off, then I'm like, "Let's see what happens; I hope it works." That's a whole different winemaking topic.

The goal of fermentation is to ferment until it is dry, which means to ferment all sugars. If it sticks (fermentation stops), you've got a problem. You can get through it, but it's a pain in the ass, and you have to work the wine too much, which could lead to a less nuanced wine.

You want to make sure the chemistry's balanced so when the yeast takes off, it can do its job; it's healthy. We inject with oxygen during that time, using medical-grade oxygen tanks. When you inject oxygen into the must, it builds stronger yeast cells early on. It will reproduce itself, rather than having a delicate yeast cell or something that'll reproduce that. We sparge with oxygen early on then we taper off. Once it starts going, we'll do one punch-down a day. Then, we'll get to two, and then we'll go back down to one. You don't overwork it; you just let it be. It's a gentle process.

During this time we'll measure it every day, temperature and brix (sugar level), to make sure that everything is on a good course. Typically, most of them are. We'll have a problem every once in a while, and we'll deal with that on the side. When it's done, we'll take off the free run, the wine that comes off the grapes, put that in a tank, and settle it overnight. Then, we'll press the must, put that in a different tank, and settle it overnight. Then we will barrel down.

We design our barrel programs based on the vineyard, and based on what tones and textures we feel the wines need. Basically, the barrels are instruments, and the wine is a song. Once the grapes are harvested, the song has been written. The barrels then can add certain tones and sounds to that song so, ultimately, the song is balanced and it sounds good.

You ferment it once in tanks, and then put it in barrels, and we ferment it again. They're different types of fermentation. The first one is the alcoholic and yeast fermentation, sugar to ethyl. The second one is malic acid to lactic acid, malolactic fermentation, which is bacterial fermentation. You want to make sure both of those are dry, dry, and dry means there's nothing left for the microbes to eat. Otherwise you may have an unstable wine.

We barrel age for fourteen to sixteen months. We overvintage, which means we hold the previous vintage in barrels through the next vintage. Takes twice as much barrel space, but it is worth it for our style. I don't like to rack the wines. Racking is when you remove the wines from the barrels, clean the barrel, then return the wine to the barrels. For me, this does a disservice to our wines and then to our blending decisions. If we rack, we will most likely introduce oxygen to the wine. To compensate for the influence of oxygen, we would need to add sulfur, more than we want to. In Pinot Noir, this can be detrimental. To use an analogy, it is like an anemone. If you slightly touch an anemone, it retracts but comes back fairly quickly. If you aggressively hit one, it does come back, but comes back injured. The same with Pinot Noir. We don't want to injure the wine; we just want to protect it. Too much aggression can take part of the soul out of the wine.

I was told early on in my winemaking evolution that the wines needed to be racked at least twice. I was not sure why but that was the way that it was done, so I thought that was what needed to be done.

So one year I didn't have time to rack our barrels. I grimaced and thought, "Oh man, I didn't rack." Then in December, when it was time to blend, I was a bit nervous. What I found out and experienced was that I had so many blending options. "Wow, these are pretty cool." I had all of these different components, and I had a color palette that I could use to craft with more accurate precision.

It's all about mouthfeel, at least that's my take on it. Once the grapes have been harvested, the aromatic and flavors are pretty much there, although they need to be protected. What we have some control over is how we ferment and what kind of barrels we use. All have an impact on the mouthfeel. I want to produce wines that hit every aspect of the palate in balance. Front of the palate to the back of the palate. Side to side and top to bottom. Movement of energy and a feeling of comfort.

We don't rack our wine so we have these different components. It makes it more complicated, but it gives us more options to fine-tune the blend. To use a music analogy, I need a cello here, an oboe there. Maybe a piccolo or a fiddle. Or maybe a bit Angus Young coming in the middle. Or some high tone Neil Peart. Make it work as it sounds best. Might not sound the best to everyone. I want it to sound good to me and hopefully others will like it too.

That's how our blending style evolved.

A lot of our winemaking experience came through trial and error, or it just presented itself. Or, I made a mistake, and it actually worked. I never would have thought of some things if I weren't a risky guy that did not know what I was doing and took certain risks.

I talked earlier about the different components that we have planned during harvest and barreling. At blending, this is where the rubber meets the road. We spend about two months blending our different lots through trials to make sure the final blend of each wine works and is as balanced as they can be—1 percent or 2 percent can make a big difference. This takes quite a bit of time and it is very fatiguing on the palate. Your palate becomes a bit worn out, so you can only taste so many wines in a given day. There are deadlines, though, as far as the bottling dates, so the work needs to be done.

There may be a wine that seems to be complete, although we can sense that a piece might be missing or something is sticking out that can throw the balance off. You have to have a bit of a crystal ball during this process to see where a wine will go after a few years in the bottle. The main thing is that the wine needs be in balance at the start. If that is the case, the wine will remain in balance throughout its life.

The process of getting the final blends to a tank for bottling is crucial. The bottle-ready wine is very susceptible to oxygen. One will be resting, and then you say to the wine, "Wake up!" The wine's response is, "Man, leave me alone." You have to be very gentle with them during this stage. It is a bit rough on the wines, although we take great care to minimize the uncomfortable factor that they will experience.

During harvest and fermentation, you can be a little rough, but they like that and need to be worked. With bottling, you have to be very gentle. You have to keep all oxygen away from the wine at all times, no matter what.

We want to get it to the tank safely, under no oxygen. You want to make sure that everything is properly sanitized. The bottling line has to be dialed in; there can't be anything on the line that is not perfectly dialed in and at a precise level of mechanism. If one thing is out of sync on the bottling line, it will throw the entire line off. The bottle sparger, the filler, the corker, the capsuler, the labeler. It all needs to work in sync. It is like running a high-end race car in a race. If one thing goes wrong, you lose the race.

For quality control on corks, make sure you get the right batches, the right corks, the right everything. Make sure that your artwork's dialed in; make sure that everything is dialed in, because there are all these pieces to the puzzle. When all that's cranking, you better make sure you have everything, and everything is in place; it's in line. Then the final check, QC, make sure the labels aren't askew. They measure by the half-millimeter. "OK, adjust if something goes out of skew and keep going." It's a pretty intense, detailed process.

I have a quick story about detail and about noticing things, being aware. What a concept. This was like ten years ago. I was at a grocery store, looking at the wine section. I was rolling down the Sauvignon Blancs and there was a local producer, big name of sizable proportion, with an upside-down label. It was on the shelf at this grocery store. OK, so this made it through the bottling line, QC, the person putting them in the cases, the person opening the cases, and the person stocking the shelves. Consumers see an upside-down label. There are a few checks and balances there that should have caught this. Obviously that did not happen. But these kinds of things happen when you become a drone. To get rid of dronedom, you rotate people around. Get people fresh, because you can't have them becoming robots and just doing the same thing all the time.

The moral of the story is that it's easy to skimp on 10 percent, but that's the difference between an 87, and a 97. That's why we got this punch-down device that's powered pneumatically. It's hard to punch down a five, eight-ton per meter by hand. I've done it. So personally speaking, I have five days, and I'm doing it for the second time today. I'm fourteen hours into my day. I'm really tired. Got that one done, next one, it's good enough. Next one, click, click. Who's looking? Done. Nobody saw that I did not get that done, so I'll start there tomorrow, and I'll catch up. It never happens.

In anything that we do, we aim for the best. Grape growing, winemaking, marketing, packaging, customer service, financing. Just to name a few. The key is the staff. That is the rocket fuel. Hire the right people, train them properly, give them the proper resources, and then get out of the way.

Then the magic happens.